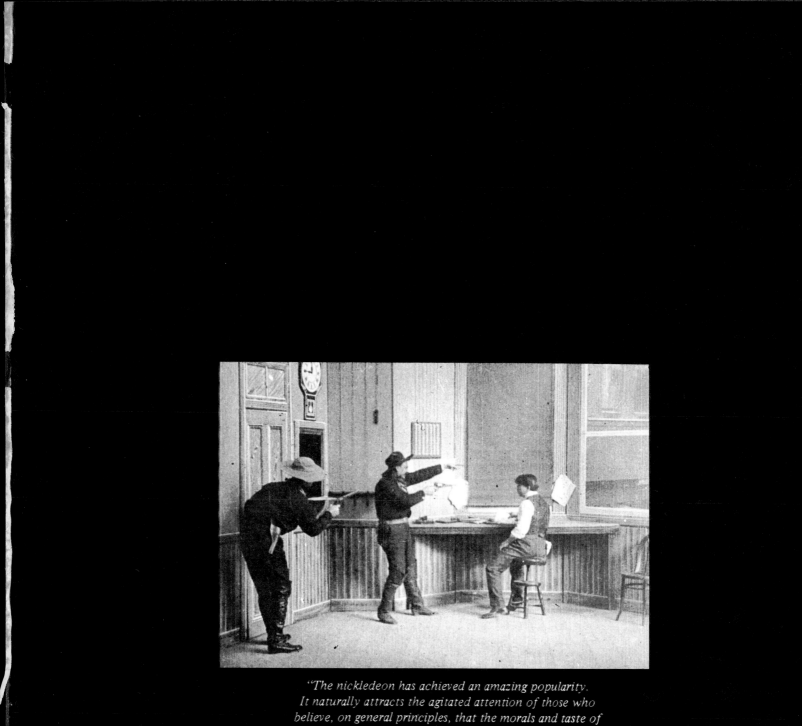

"The nickledeon has achieved an amazing popularity.
It naturally attracts the agitated attention of those who
believe, on general principles, that the morals and taste of
the lowly always need looking after."

THE SATURDAY EVENING POST

MOVIE BOOK

©1977
The Curtis Publishing Company
Indianapolis, Indiana

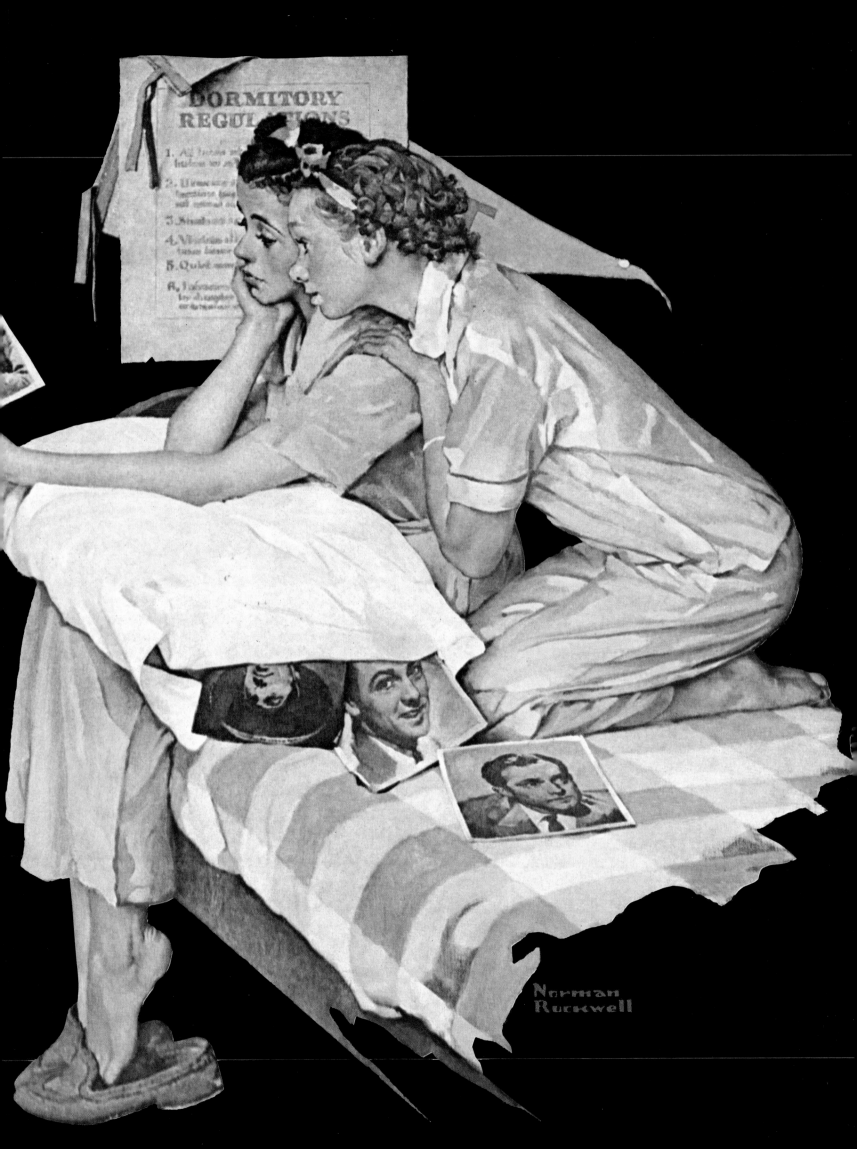

*"To serve equally two masters, the box office and the critic,
is the unique and spectacular goal of American cinema."*

The Saturday Evening Post 1977

The Curtis Publishing Company

Chairman
Beurt SerVaas

Co-Chairman
Cory SerVaas

Staff for *The Saturday Evening Post Movie Book*

Designer
Don Moldroski

Editor-in-Chief
Starkey Flythe, Jr.

Managing Editors
Thom Satrom, David Bumke

Editorial Staff
**Jan Brewer, Jean White, Barbara Davis,
John J. Rea, Anna C. McAndrews, Kathryn Klassen**

Copy Staff
Astrid Henkels, Louise Fortson

Art Staff
**Steve Miller, Kay Douglas, Jinny Sauer,
Dwight E. Lamb, Marianne Sullivan**

President, Curtis Book Division
Jack Merritt

Production Manager, Curtis Book Division
David M. Price

Production Staff
**Marie Caldwell, Geri Watson, Gloria McCoy,
Penny Allison, Rose Thompson**

Contents

Projecting Shapes in Light

The movies are a confessional of dreams. Audiences sit in dark rows and proclaim in roaring silence their desires for romance and adventure, for heroism and glamour and power and beauty.

No politician, no king is as well known as the movie star of the moment. And no history, no matter how well written or beautifully painted, is as perfectly packaged and profusely illustrated as a movie.

That movie is fashion, speech, mores, science, art, industry—a mirror of our time and our emotions—set down for all time in the amber of celluloid.

The movies have been wonderfully free of pretension. Their early comic masters saw the medium as living art, a storehouse for motion and action, not a museum for dialectic. Even today, documentaries must dwell within their own categories and box office is always a more certain prediction of permanence than critical or artistic acclaim.

The film has been called an American art form. It is a technical art form, and technical excellence is taken for granted by American audiences and, by extension, world audiences. So-called artistic effects are often hooted down by theatergoers or at best confused with trouble in the projection room. H. L. Mencken's dictum that no one ever went broke underestimating the taste of the American public has nowhere proven more wrong than in the movies. *Birth of a Nation, Gone With the Wind, The Grapes of Wrath, The Godfather* drew record crowds as well as record awards.

Mary Pickford once noted with regret the passing of the silent film because talkies would abolish a universal language. The passionate and dramatic movements of the great silent screen stars passed out of the ken of new actors and a grunt often replaced a flashing eye or graceful gesture.

The movies have followed the migrations of our population. From downtown to the suburbs the movie houses have moved with their audiences. The great Hispano-Moresque palaces, which once got people in the mood for exotic adventures much as flights of steps get people in the frame of mind for art at museums or Doric columns make them think Roman for banking, gave way to metal utility buildings, suburban in principle, designed to store audiences rather than enchant them.

For a time in the 1940s, movie theaters were almost forums where worthy causes chose to greet and solicit from the American public both on screen and off. The actors were enlisted to work for the program—often something like the March of Dimes or the Heart Fund—and the straw baskets were passed like offertory plates in a church. But the theaters soon found charitable moods might better be turned to the concession stand. Prices went up and popcorn, de rigueur for darkness where sex wasn't involved, began to rival the price of admission.

Money and movies have ever been companionable bedfellows. Stars have always commanded salaries to make the President, Mayor and Governor look like candidates for welfare, and big-budget movies guarantee advance publicity. Making movies is hard work, but Bette Davis once noted you could always tell when a star was washed up because she went back to Broadway. Now that was work. You might have to get up at five a.m. and be on the set at four to make movies, but there was a shooting schedule and you weren't on stage for the entire movie and they could splice your better moments with your best. And when it was all over you had a voice and your health and a fat piece of the royalties, and the film was permanent, whereas the playgoers remembered you on the night they happened to see you, possibly not your greatest, and parts were few and far between, especially if you were a star. Or if you weren't.

Television's impact on movies has been curious. Movies are made now solely for TV, and "The Late Show" has introduced the great films of the twenties, thirties, and forties to new audiences who have come to worship the old faces to the point of adorning their T-shirts with their glamorous images.

Television stars are perhaps better known to American audiences than movie stars, but one television star has observed a strange lack of respect for TV people compared to the denizens of the film. "They think because you've been in their living rooms, they can take any liberty with you," says a veteran of ten years in television. "But they seem in awe of movie stars." "Once," says Carol Burnett, "I came downstairs in my house and some fans were going through the kitchen." It seems unlikely, however, that movie stars would even have kitchens in their Valentino-esque falcons' lairs or that we, mere mortals, could ever discover exactly where these screen sirens lived.

To become eternal, movie stars were willing, when time tolled its fateful knell, to endure facial surgery, killing exercises and to obscure the original premise of their

Early movie palaces mirrored the flamboyant lifestyles of the "Golden Age" stars who made the featured attractions. Their movies and lives gave a depression-saddled nation valuable distraction.

appearance with new eyebrows, noses, chins and hair lines. Lights and makeup and lace curtains in front of the camera helped, too, for unlike the English cinema, becoming a character actress seemed a fate worse than death. Unless the actress did it early enough in her career and could go back to an image of glamour, i.e. Elizabeth Taylor in *Who's Afraid of Virginia Woolf?*

Like the fiction of stars' faces, the fictions of plot and action became the facts of history and we remember more of the Civil War from *Gone With the Wind* than from textbooks in school; we know William Randolph Hearst and Huey Long and the force and bite of power from *Citizen Kane* and *All the King's Men,* not from their records in public life. Was it not part of the learning process, for us as well as for him, that Hearst *became* a movie, chose a mate from the screen, built his own set, sat there in his castle and watched, night after night, movies, movies, movies. Running for Senate or Governor was one thing, but watching movies was the life, the life that only the wealthiest art could afford. Howard Hughes found dabbling in the movies more exhilarating than flying. Joseph P. Kennedy discovered the yellow brick road to his sons' destinies in Hollywood. Hollywood was a dreamland in reverse in those years, a light and revelation to the reality of the public mind.

But it is not the great names who have made the movies the most popular of the popular arts. It is the humble. The mixed-up foundling, Norma Jean Baker, who in the end knew her psychiatrist better than her fans. Elvis Presley,

the country boy with the guitar who knew he couldn't last if he fulfilled the promises to his followers. The real cowboys who became movie star cowboys and always thought it was a little sissyish.

At the Museum of Modern Art in New York, curators say that Greta Garbo used to watch her old movies and murmur to herself as if she were a third person, "Look at her, now she's going to ask him for a drink." It would be like that, and Presley and Jean Harlow and Marilyn Monroe and James Dean and Montgomery Clift must've been frightened by the disparity between their living portraits as stars and the reality of their lives. Perhaps their art was not pervasive enough to sustain them—unlike the painter's or writer's art, it does not encourage pleasure in history (the history of the cinema is a recent preoccupation with young people) and because of the notoriety the movies affords its practitioners, loneliness is a fact of existence. It has been difficult to distinguish between public relations gimmicks and sincerity. Hollywood stars have complained, but few have been willing to give up their careers for privacy and many seem almost in love with the love of their fans.

The movies began simply. Many of the first sets and situations were simply mirrors held, however unsteadily, up to nature. The grand and glorious spectacles arrived early and persisted, but honest emotion, conveyable and digestible when received by the audience, remains the staple. Humor, pathos, happiness, possibility—these are the great ingredients of great movies.

Moviemaking remains an art of technique. Many stage successes—both people and vehicles—do not translate well into movies. The camera must conceal its style to demonstrate it. Actor and actress must wiggle their way into the

Elizabeth Taylor and James Dean in **Giant.** *Taylor brought the movies to heel with a colossal career; Dean's success swerved out of control like the car that killed him.*

tiniest place in your heart and brain in order to be really grand. Music has to come from a background so remote it does not compete with your sigh. The lighting should tell the time but not be hard on your eyes. Direction should alter that which is natural without making it appear altered; the favorite stars are those who are "just like real people"—the best actors and directors know how difficult that is. And producers are best when they conceal their budgets. The story must move along yet the audience mustn't be hurried, and in the end we must know the characters and care about them. And this difficult chariot of talent and story and emotion must run as cleanly and effortlessly as a fine automobile, only you should not be aware of the ticking of the electric clock. That is technique. That is a good movie.

And *The Saturday Evening Post Movie Book* is about good movies. And a few bad ones. And the people who made them and watched them and loved them.

"Art and life are different, which is why we call one art and the other life," said Goethe. Art, here as the camera, deals with life, Teresa Wright in **Shadow of a Doubt.**

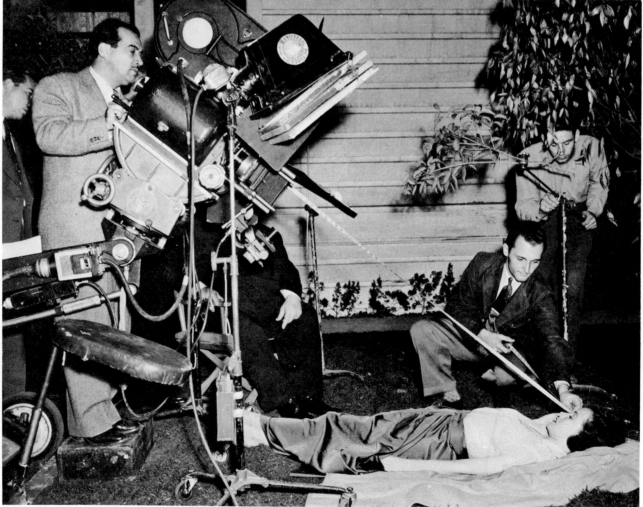

Patents, Profits and Pirates

by Thomas A. Edison

I began working upon motion pictures after looking over the toy called a zoetrope, or wheel of life. You can find them in any toy store. Pictures of a series of figures showing fractional parts of the motion of an object, like a boy skating, are put on a strip of paper. The paper is placed inside a cylinder. The cylinder is on a pivot and can be revolved. Then the figures on the paper seem to be in motion when viewed through the openings. My experiments with this philosophical toy are told in W. H. Meadowcroft's *Boys' Life of Edison*. Mr. Meadowcroft has long been my assistant in the laboratory.

After prolonged experimentation, I concluded that if the art of producing motion pictures was ever to be reduced to practice and commercialized, a camera would have to be made possessing these features:

FIRST. A single lens viewing the scene from a single and fixed point of view, like the human eye, instead of using several lenses as others had done.

SECOND. A long, tapelike sensitive film moving intermittently with respect to the lens and rapidly enough to utilize persistence of vision.

THIRD. A shutter for instantaneously exposing the film at each minute period of rest.

All these essential features were finally worked out in the laboratory, and it was absolutely the first machine for taking motion pictures ever put together which embraced the requirements for the ultimate and permanent success of the enterprise. And, even then, my pictures were far from perfect. There was too much flicker. Honestly, I was puzzled and a little bit disgusted.

About that time a man named Armat—Thomas Armat, now a wealthy and prominent resident of Washington, D.C.—came along with a remedy for that flicker trouble. Finally, I said to him, "All right, Armat, come along with your ideas, and we'll put yours with mine and perfect the darn thing"—and we did. Armat's help had to do with the projection of the picture. My camera for taking the pictures was sound in every particular.

We opened up the first night at Keith's Colonial Thea-

ter—now the Walter Hampden Theater—in New York City, on February 13, 1913. I am reminded of the date by Samuel Tauber, then manager of that theater, who quite recently grew reminiscent for the *New York Times* and told some funny stories about having passed out the word, after the manner of theatrical managers, that "Mr. Edison, in person, would be present," and then had a hard time explaining my failure to come before the curtain and make a speech when the audience called for me.   *(1930)*

Edison had over 1,000 patents. He believed motion pictures would extend man's day and his mind—as had his other creations, the electric light and phonograph.

Drama by the Foot
by Valentine Karlyn

The day when we were pleasantly surprised by the kinetoscopic presentation of such ordinary events as the arrival and departure of railway trains or the coming and going of the crowds on the boardwalk of Atlantic City is over. Making a moving picture now involves more or less creative effort.

It is doubtful if the theatrical managers of the world have ever so carefully felt the pulse of the great public as have the men who make moving pictures. The multitude undeniably gets what it wants. It likes melodrama and farce, and accordingly there is no end of film plays in which the villains are foiled by beautiful heroines and handsome heroes, and in which awkward men make themselves ridiculous. Variety is the spice of the moving-picture show. Change, change and change again is what the moving-picture groundlings crave. They get it as they can never get it in the most kaleidoscopic melodrama, the tawdriest novel, or the yellowest of yellow journals.

Current events are often drawn upon to furnish the subjects of the most popular films.

To reproduce the storming of San Juan Hill a battle was fought in the Orange Mountains. *The Great Train Robbery,* a film that cost $20,000, was taken in part near Paterson, New Jersey, with the assistance of a specially-engaged train and a company of one hundred men and women to act as passengers, train-crew and bandits. One filmmaker conceived the idea of reproducing Custer's last fight, and to that end he brought a band of Sioux Indians from the West, among whom were three chiefs who had actually participated in the tragedy that cost Custer and 300 of his men their lives. Is it any wonder that the people who live near moving-picture studios are hardened to battle scenes, earthquakes, riots and cowboy exploits?

The stage manager reigns supreme. His slightest mandate, usually colored with picturesque, impatient epithets, is obeyed as if he were a captain drilling a company of soldiers. Often the actors know nothing of the plot. The stage manager rehearses the play scene by scene, ten or a dozen times. When the characters are sufficiently drilled he gives the word, "Ready for the picture," and the players perform their parts as the camera shutter clicks. The camera operator rarely has an opportunity of turning the crank for any length of time, so exacting, rigorous and pedantically fussy is the stage manager. Scenes are repeated over and over again, and yards of film are destroyed before he is satisfied. A hundred feet of film may represent a morning's hard work and perhaps a whole day's work.

Curiously enough, the actors and actresses must talk, for sound is apparently necessary to express human emotions. The villain in a photographic melodrama cannot help hissing "Cur-r-rse you!" into the shrinking heroine's ear, nor can the hero refrain from shouting "By Heaven, I *will* save her!" although the millions that will see him on the screen will never thrill at the words.   *(1909)*

The Civil War was the great event of living memory for early filmmakers. Harvard's President Lowell roundly censured D. W. Griffith, a Georgian, for his interpretation in **The Birth of a Nation.** *Boston theaters were picketed, but emotions in the film transcended regional boundaries.*

Ambassadors

by Mary Pickford

Douglas and I—I refer, of course, to Douglas Fairbanks, my husband—were concluding our seventh trip abroad. We had gone to Switzerland, where my little niece had been placed in school, and instead of returning as before, over the Atlantic, we decided to roam back through Egypt, India, China and Japan, and thence to Los Angeles over the Pacific.

On previous trips to Europe we had had some hectic and thrilling experiences with street mobs—particularly in London and Moscow. Somehow we counted upon this new journey into Northern Africa and the Far East as one on which we could go as we pleased, unobserved and free willed. But it was not to be so. It turned, increasingly, into the most remarkable reception we have ever had. We rarely knew our own plans ahead, from one embarkation to another; and, once decided upon, we tried faithfully to keep the news to ourselves. But, somehow or other, the word went winging ahead.

I shall never forget the dismay, and then the utter indignation, of Karl Kitchen, newspaper writer, who happened to be with us when our train pulled into Kyoto and the mob at the station engulfed us. I was rescued just in time and sat perched upon Douglas' shoulders until the mounted police, with drawn sabers, cleared a lane for us. Poor Mr. Kitchen was thrown down and trampled over. When he got to his feet he sent his fists swinging right and left. When, after a violent struggle, we finally reached our rooms at the hotel by way of a rear elevator, the disheveled Mr. Kitchen exclaimed:

"This is outrageous! How can you keep taking it with a smile?"

I talked to him for some time. "This is cordiality," I said. "A great expression of friendliness. Stop and think—what a remarkable tribute to the motion picture."

I shall always remember an experience in Spain. Douglas and I had attended a race meet, at which were present King Alphonso, the Queen Mother and the Queen of Portugal. As we passed through the gate a beggar woman darted through the crowd and plucked my sleeve.

I turned, expecting the usual request for alms, but something in the swarthy, wrinkled face made me pause and listen. In a torrent of Spanish the poor old woman was telling me that my pictures warmed her heart—that she would hold this a gala day in her life because she had seen and touched me.

Later in the afternoon, the Queen of Portugal, learning that we were present, sent for us. I can see her now, all in black, a regal figure, the shadow of her sorrows upon her fine face. She bowed deeply as I stood before her, and in a manner so formal as to make an oration of her kindly words, said: "Through all my dark days of heartache you have been a ray of light. Your pictures have been my only pleasure and diversion."

I stood there, I am afraid, too long silent with the realization that a queen was saying what I had just heard from the lips of a beggar. *(1930)*

Doug and Mary and Chaplin founded United Artists, brought Shakespeare and shenanigans to movies with dazzling brilliance, perfected pantomime in films.

Pickfair's Doug

by Joseph Hergesheimer

There was nothing humanly possible, from the most trivial dexterity to a final beauty of complete balance, that Douglas Fairbanks couldn't do with his body.

When I had seen him before, he was practicing the airy flipping of a cigarette from his palm to his mouth; and now, in the interest of *Don Q*, he had mastered the long, incredibly wicked cattle-driving whip of Australia and Spain. It was composed of a short rigid stock and a flexible whip and lash, twelve feet long anyhow: standing lightly, Douglas cracked it, a single and then a double report, as sharp and loud and as dangerous as the explosion of a heavy rifle. Then, in the way of variety, he picked a flower from the bright border along the porch; the whip cut it without disturbing a leaf, hardly moving its stem. Douglas cut in half heavy stakes set in a stump; the whip broke sixteen thicknesses of wood; he slashed the cigarette from the lips of a young man with steady nerves and the nicest confidence in Douglas' skill.

I took it from him; it was utterly dead and inert. A futile inept movement did nothing, but a stronger resentful effort brought the lash across my face; a third trial tied the whip very effectually about my legs, and I gave it up. It needs a lot of practice, Douglas observed. *(1926)*

Fairbanks' good looks and energetic gymnastics created the star system and brought the swashbuckler from Denver fame, money and love.

Among the Stars

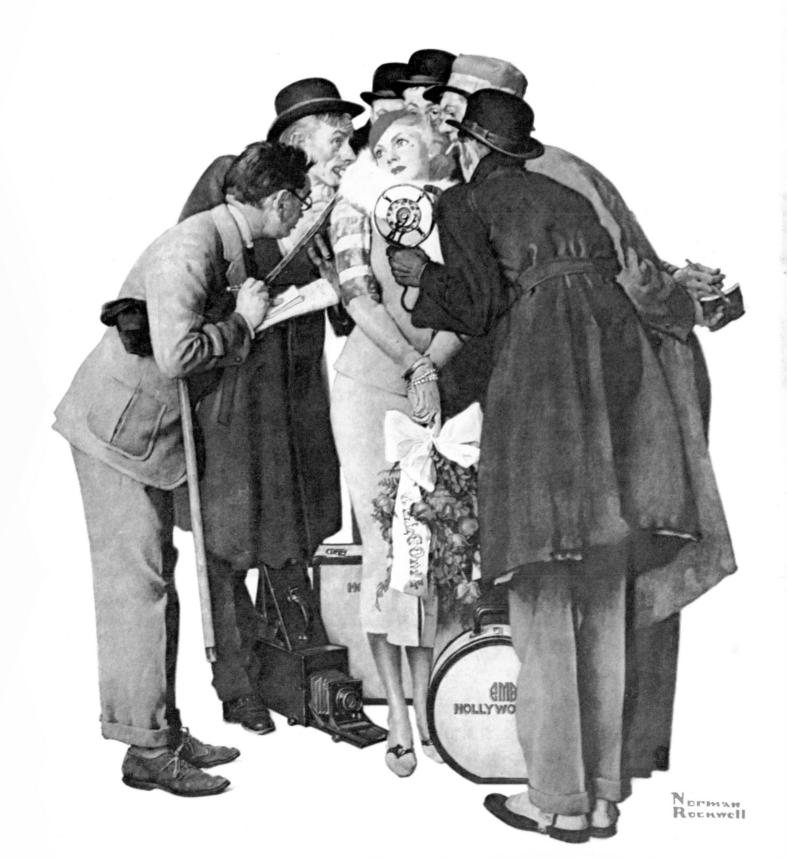

Pete Martin

When Pete Martin was six years old, he diverted a nickel destined for the Sunday school collection plate into a ticket for the movies. From that moment Martin believed in movie stars, saw them as real people, employees in an industry rather than dream merchants. When he became a writer, he perfected the Hollywood interview. His tape recorder was all ears, and stars shed to Pete secrets their psychiatrists would never know. Still, his stories, according to the movies' number one writer, Nunnally Johnson, were "some of the truest and fairest about Hollywood ever published." Gable gave Martin a taped interview, the only one he ever made. Gary Cooper "opened up as if I'd pulled a plug out of a rusty tank." Taping made Marilyn Monroe so nervous Martin wrote the interview out in long hand. He wrote Crosby's story and Hope's. Bing staked out a watch and observed Martin for a half hour to make sure he was the right Boswell. Pete remembers his "washed denim-blue eyes boring right through me." When Martin did Arthur Godfrey's story for the magazine, 750,000 additional copies were sold. Everybody liked it except Godfrey, who said, "If you think I'm going to sign my name to that, you're crazy." So Godfrey rewrote Martin and Martin's editors put it all back and the readers loved it. Jimmy Stewart's drawl took an extra 20 pages over the usual two-hour tape. Pete knew Ingrid Bergman would "dry up" if he took out his notebook, so he memorized the interview and shut his eyes to avoid distractions on the way back to Philadelphia, where he sat up all night typing his memories. There is nothing grand in Martin's style. His style is his subject's. That is what *Post* readers wanted. And that was what made Martin the master visitor.

"It makes me nervous to see that thing going round," said Monroe of Pete's tape machine. "Never mind how nervous she made me," swallowed Pete.

The King

It has taken me three years to write this story. It's not the way it was supposed to be originally, but it's still a story no one has ever told—and it has been told to me by the one who knows it best, Clark Gable. The idea had been for Gable to give me a detailed play-by-play of his entire life. A mutual friend, Howard Strickling, brought us together in 1954 in his backyard at Encino, out in the San Fernando Valley.

Howard said helpfully, "Tell him about that screwball paternity suit, Clark." And Gable had told me. We worked out a method of tackling our projected writing job. "We'll put it all down; then we'll cut out anything that might hurt anybody," Gable said. I said that was fine with me.

It shaped up as a pleasant assignment. Gable was forthright, down to earth, easy to get along with, at least 200 percent male.

When we said good-bye, he said, "Give me a month to think it over," and I said, "Sure."

Three years intervened. I dropped in on Bing Crosby and spent a couple of hours yakking with him about anything that popped into our heads. I asked questions and he answered them if he felt like it, and in the way he felt like answering them. When Gable read that interview, he sent me a message. I was told, "If you want to do it that way, he's game."

"I'll be there," I said.

When Gable walked into my hotel room, he wore no safari clothes. His dark suit fitted faultlessly.

"You ask me questions and I'll tell you the truth," he told me. "If you ask me something too personal, I'll say, 'That's a question I don't care to answer; I'm keeping that to myself.' But if you ask me something that I feel I can answer honestly, I will."

"I've never forgotten a couple of the stories you told me that afternoon around Howard's pool," I said. "There was that anecdote you told me about a threatened paternity suit," I reminded him.

"That started slowly," he said, "then it built. I got a letter or two, at my home, from a woman in Canada. She asked me if she could see me about a personal matter. I had never heard of her, so I ignored her, but her letters kept on arriving just the same.

"She finally said I would remember her because she had been in England in such and such a year, that I'd had an affair with her then, and, as a result of that affair, a child had been born. Her letters said she thought something should be done about providing for the child.

"At the time she said all this happened, I'd never been in England. I'd never been out of North America—so I'd never had a United States passport. As affairs go, the one she described was a long-distance project. It must have set a world's record, so I decided she was nuts and forgot about it.

"Then Walter Winchell began to get letters from her about me. And letters also began to arrive at my studio, M-G-M, and Winchell and the studio asked, 'What is all this?'

"As I remember it, I was told by the United States district attorney in Los Angeles that his office had heard about those letters, and he sent an assistant United States district attorney to see me. He told me, 'You'll not only have to prove that you weren't in England when this child was conceived; you'll have to prove where you actually were at that time. Can you do it?'

" 'It's not going to be easy,' I said. 'When the woman who wrote those letters said I was in England, I was pretty much of a wandering trouper. I was in shows and out of shows and working in lumber camps.' But with this threat in mind I reached back into my memory and I was able to prove where I'd been. I came up with two kinds of proof: old, dated theater programs with my name on them, and pay checks made out to me by the Silverton Lumber Company, in Silverton, Oregon. When I was supposed to be in England, I had been piling lumber in Oregon for three dollars and twenty cents a day.

"The postal authorities had the woman indicted for using the mails to defraud."

"I don't see how you could have avoided playing Rhett Butler in *Gone With the Wind*," I said. "The whole country cast you in it long before the cameras began to roll."

"That was exactly the trouble," Gable said. "Not only that, but it seemed to me that the public's casting was being guided by an elaborate publicity campaign.

"My thinking about it was this; that novel was one of the all-time best-sellers. People didn't just read it, they lived it. They visualized its characters, and they formed passionate convictions about them. You say a lot of people thought I ought to play Rhett Butler, but I didn't know how many had formed that opinion."

"Enough," I said.

"There are never enough," he told me. "But one thing was certain: they had a preconceived idea of the kind of Rhett Butler they were going to see, and suppose I came up empty?"

"But you did produce," I said.

"Maybe so," he said noncommittally.

"When did you finally get it through your head you'd done all right?"

He said, "The night we opened in Atlanta, I said, 'I guess this movie is in.' "

"How did you figure that?" I asked. "Did you enjoy it yourself, listen to the critics, or did you gauge it by other people's reactions?"

"Other people's reactions," he told me.

"I can't figure whether it was Darryl Zanuck or Irving Thalberg who took a look at your ears and thumbed you down as an actor."

"Darryl and Irving both did that at different times," Gable said. "Darryl was head of production at Warner Brothers. I don't know his story, but I do know the Thalberg 'ears' story. I'd been the juvenile lead in *The Copperhead*, with Lionel Barrymore, in Los Angeles, but I couldn't seem to cut the mustard in pictures, so I went to New York and found work on the stage. While I was there, Lionel became a director at M-G-M. Later I came back to Hollywood in *The Last Mile*, and Lionel came to the old Majestic Theater to see me in it. He came backstage afterward and said, 'Come on out to the studio. I want you to make a screen test.'

" 'No use,' I said. 'I've tried working in pictures. They don't want me.'

" 'Wait a minute,' he said; 'there's a thing called sound in pictures now, and these actors out here can't talk. You can.' I went out to M-G-M and Lionel said, 'Go over to makeup.' I went over and they curled my hair."

He bent his head and I could see the natural wave in his hair. "You see how much I need a curl," he said, "but they curled it anyhow. Then I went over to wardrobe, where they stripped me and gave me a G-string. The sound stage where they were making the test was a long way off. I'm no exhibitionist and I was embarrassed making that trek all the way to the sound stage.

"When I showed up on that M-G-M sound stage," Gable

The intellectual sensitivity of Leslie Howard's heroism was strikingly contrasted with Gable's slightly gamblerish roughness. Miss Leigh managed both types.

said, "I asked Lionel, 'What is this? Why am I curly-haired and half naked?'

" 'I'm directing *The Bird of Paradise*,' he told me. 'I want you to play the native boy in it.' A prop man stuck a hibiscus behind one of my ears, shoved a knife in my G-string, and there I was, creeping through the bushes, looking for a girl. Lionel had made a big thing out of 'these actors out here can't talk,' but he'd given me nothing to say throughout the test. Then my test was sent in for Irving Thalberg to look at. He called Lionel in and said, 'You can't put this man in a picture. Look at him!'

"Lionel said loyally, 'He's a good stage actor. He's young, but he'll be all right.' Irving Thalberg said, 'Not for my money he won't be all right. Look at his big, batlike ears.' "

"What do you think about television?" I said. "Do you have any reticences about that subject?"

"I can tell you in a very few words what I think about it," he said. "I don't want any of it."

"Why?" I asked.

"It's hurting a profession I'm very grateful to—motion pictures," he said. "TV is here, and I know it's not going away, but I'm going to help as much as I can to keep the picture business strong as long as I can. I owe motion pictures that much, as well as the people who have worked in them with me for years. Television is fine, but as a medium of entertainment I don't think it's in the same class with motion pictures. Not with that tiny screen. I'm still a motion-picture personality and I intend to stay one as long as I'm around."   *(1957)*

Clean-shaven in his earliest movies, Gable used a mustache and Jean Harlow in Red Dust *(1932) to become Louis B. Mayer's most valuable—though not most obedient—star.*

Tragedy in Blonde

"Pictures of you usually show you with mouth open and your eyes half closed. Did some photographer sell you the idea that having your picture taken that way makes you look sexier?"

She replied in what I'd come to recognize as pure Monroese. "The formation on my lids must make them look heavy or else I'm thinking of something," she told me. "Sometimes I'm thinking of men. Other times I'm thinking of some man in particular. It's easier to look sexy when you're thinking of some man in particular. As for my mouth being open all the time, I even sleep with it open. I know, because it's open when I wake up. I never consciously think of my mouth, but I do consciously think about what I'm thinking about."

When I asked her, "Has anyone ever accused you of wearing falsies?" she came through with a genuine Monroeism.

"Yes," she told me, her eyes flashing indignantly. "Naturally," she went on, "it was another actress who accused me. My answer to that is, quote: Those who know me better know better. That's all. Unquote."

Another Monroeism followed hard on the heels of that. I said, "I've heard that you wowed the marines in Korea when you climbed up onto a platform to say a few words to them, and they whistled at you and made wolf calls."

"I know the time you're talking about," she said. "It wasn't in Korea at all; it was at Camp Pendleton, California. They wanted me to say a few words, so I said, 'You fellows down there are always whistling at sweater girls. Well, take away their sweaters and what have you got?' For some reason they screamed and yelled."

Still another Monroeism had emerged from a press conference in the Plaza Hotel, in New York City. It was held to announce her teaming with Sir Laurence Olivier in an acting-directing-producing venture—a get-together described by one of those present as "one of the least likely duos in cinematic history." The big Monroeism of that occasion was Marilyn's answer to the query, "Miss Monroe, do you still want to do *The Brothers Karamazov* on Broadway?"

"I don't want to play The Brothers," she said. "I want to play Grushenka from that book. She's a girl."

Billy Wilder, the Hollywood director who directed Marilyn in *The Seven Year Itch*, is witty, also pungent, pithy, and is not afraid to say what he thinks. "When you come right down to it," Wilder told me, "that calendar is not repulsive. It's quite lovely. Marilyn's name was already pretty big when the calendar story broke. If it hadn't been, nobody would have cared one way or the other. But when it became known that she had posed for

it, I think that, if anything, it helped her popularity. It appealed to people who like to read about millionaires who started life selling newspapers on the corner of Forty-second and Fifth Avenue. It was as if Marilyn had been working her way through college. Here was a girl who needed dough, and she made it by honest toil."

"I was working on the Fox Western Avenue lot when this worried man from Fox came tearing in wringing his hands," Marilyn told me recently. "He took me into my dressing room to talk about the horrible thing I'd done in posing for such a photograph. I could think of nothing else to say, so I said apologetically, 'I thought the lighting the photographer used would disguise me.' I thought that worried man would have a stroke when I told him that.

"What had happened was I was behind in my rent at the Hollywood Studio Club, where girls stay who hope to crash the movies. A lot of photographers had asked me to pose in the nude, but I'd always said, 'No.' I was getting five dollars an hour for plain modeling, but the price for nude modeling was fifty an hour. So I called Tom Kelley, a photographer I knew, and said, 'They're kicking me out of here. How soon can we do it?' He said, 'We can do it tomorrow.'

"I didn't even have to get dressed, so it didn't take long. I mean it takes longer to get dressed than it does to get undressed. I'd asked Tom, 'Please don't have anyone else there except your wife, Natalie.' He said, 'O.K.' He only made two poses. There was a shot of me sitting up and a shot of me lying down. I think the one of me lying down is the best.

"I'm saving a copy of that calendar for my grandchildren," Marilyn went on, all bright-eyed.

I asked Marilyn herself if she thought that then-husband Joe DiMaggio had disapproved of her skirts blowing around her shoulders in *The Seven Year Itch*. I said I had heard his reaction described in two ways: that he had been furious and that he had taken it calmly.

"One of those two is correct," Marilyn said. "Maybe you can figure it out for yourself if you'll give it a little thought."

Something told me that, in her opinion, Joe had been very annoyed indeed. And while we were on the subject of Joe, it seemed a good time to find out about how things had been between them when they had been married, and the unbelievable scene which accompanied the breaking up of that marriage.

When I brought the subject up, Marilyn said, "For a

Director Billy Wilder was aware of Marilyn's "flesh impact." She was never lost or invisible.

Marilyn with columnist Walter Winchell. He appeared in four movies but was replaced in a fifth by Rosalind Russell (these things happen in Hollywood).

man and a wife to live intimately together is not an easy thing at best. If it's not just exactly right in every way it's practically impossible, but I'm still optimistic." She sat there being optimistic. Then she said, with feeling, "However, I think TV sets should be taken out of the bedroom."

"Did you and Joe have one in your bedroom?" I asked.

"No comment," she said emphatically. "But everything I say to you I speak from experience. You can make what you want of that."

She was quiet for a moment; then she said, "When I showed up in divorce court to get my divorce from Joe, there were mobs of people there asking me bunches of questions. And they asked, 'Are you and Joe still friends?' and I said, 'Yes, but I still don't know anything about baseball.' And they all laughed. I don't see what was so funny. I'd heard that he was a fine baseball player, but I'd never seen him play."   *(1956)*

At the Stork Club in happier days, Marilyn and second husband, baseball great Joe DiMaggio.

Monroe and Gable on the set of The Misfits. *In the background: Arthur Miller.*

That Man Cooper

If, as some of the tougher and more gristle-minded students of Hollywood believe, success, instead of failure, is that community's unforgivable sin, Gary Cooper is one of its greatest sinners. Since he appeared in *The Winning of Barbara Worth*, in 1927, he has switched on his slow grin and his special brand of hard-to-ignite masculinity in sixty-three movies. Among them they have grossed enough millions—160 in all—to impress even a Texas oil baron whose wife buys her mink coats by the gross.

In 1940, Gary's salary was the largest paid to anyone in the United States. It was the first time a movie star had pulled down the nation's heaviest sugar.

As if all this were not a diet of triumphs too rich to be digested by Cooper's rivals who've never eaten that high off the hog, popular acclaim has also dubbed him with a kind of knighthood, an extra helping of glory, which gives many of those who have not been so honored incurable cases of heartburn. *The New York Times* has called him "the incorruptible Galahad of moviedom."

But I hadn't worked long on the Cooper story before I ran into a wholly unexpected amount of Cooper back-stabbing and belittling. These word battles between Cooper's defenders and those who delight in giving him a verbal hosing usually begin with a query such as the following: "Can he act?"

I am a charter-member Cooper addict myself, and such cynicism upset me. So I decided to drop in on a bubble-shaped man named Jack Moss, who at one time had been Cooper's business manager, and put the "Can he act?" question to him.

"That," he told me, "is an enigma that has baffled some of the best brains in picture business. It even temporarily stopped a top-notch director we'll call Jones."

As Moss told it, when Jones directed Gary in one of his most successful pictures, he began to shoot the film on a Monday. The following Thursday, Jones called Moss on the phone to ask, "Can you come right over?" From the tone of his voice, Moss could tell that Jones was unhappy. When he got there, the director led him to one side, where they could be alone. "What's wrong with this Cooper, anyhow?" Jones asked. "He's not only dead on his feet, his face is dead too. Doesn't he sleep nights?"

"He sleeps fine, nights," Moss said.

"Then why does nothing happen when he's up there in front of the camera? All I get out of him is a blank look. He's ruining me!"

"Coop doesn't give like other actors," Moss reminded Jones soothingly. "He doesn't shoot off emotions like a Roman candle." Then he inquired, "Have you looked at the footage you've already shot?"

"What's that got to do with it?" Jones asked. "I never look at my rushes the first week."

"You'd better look at these," Moss told him. "I can only tell you that when the light reflected from Coop's face hits the raw emulsion on film something happens. I don't know what it is."

Jones broke his rule and looked at his first week's rushes. His anxiety evaporated. On the projection-room screen he saw the astute underplaying that later helped him cop an award for a good job of directing.

Hollywood's habit of sneering at Cooper's acting annoys fellow actor Walter Brennan. "When it comes to technique, his is effortless," he said. "And for that reason, it's one of the best. All of his seeming carelessness and his apparent nonacting is carefully studied out and is beautifully done. He may have only one trick—that of being natural and relaxed—but it's one of the hardest tricks for an actor to do."

The classic tale of Gary's ability to relax concerns the filming of a scene in which the audience was supposed to think he had been catapulted from an automobile during a smashup. Told to simulate unconsciousness in a snowdrift while the camera peered down at him, he took his position on a mound of corn-flake snow. The director called, "Let 'er roll!" and, when Cooper had been photographed from several angles, yelled, "Cut!" Gary kept right on lying in the corn flakes. He had fallen fast asleep.

The hotly debated question, "Is Cooper's conversation limited to 'ughs' or can he actually talk when the sound track's not listening?" still remained for me to investigate. Among the stories repeated to me was one involving Slim Talbot. For years Talbot served as Gary's stand-in. In that time Gary was said to have spoken fewer than 200 words to him. Cooper and Slim had shared a tent on location in Arizona. One night when a sandstorm began to blow, they'd rushed out to hold the tent down, and Slim had yelled, "Big blow, ain't it?" For hours they battled flapping canvas, until a violent gust tore it from their hands. As they ran for the nearest shelter, Gary is said to have shouted, "Sure is!"

When he donned a full-dress uniform for *The Lives of a Bengal Lancer*, the makeup department took a horrified look at his shanks and wrapped yards of bandages around them, hoarsely muttering, "More muscle, more muscle." Cooper's knees are said to be the sharpest in Hollywood. After perching on his lap throughout most of a long day's shooting, Claudette Colbert rubbed her dented derriere

Norman Rockwell in a 1930 Post *cover catches a moment of whimsey as Gary Cooper, playing a rough-and-tough cowpuncher, gets prettied up for a Western.*

and remarked, "Mother should have told me there'd be days like this."

But not all of Cooper's contacts with women have made them so rueful, for the sedately married Cooper of 1950 was once party to some pretty torrid romances. His helplessness as a screen lover seemed to strengthen a number of ladies in their determination to tutor him in the tender arts, and once they got the range, he didn't escape the lacy nets flung at him. Recalling one of those damsels during her attachment for Gary, another Hollywood woman remarked, "All I can say is that when she was that way about him, she was more that way than any other woman I've ever known."

Adela Rogers St. Johns described another Cooper collector by saying. "Having her fall in love with you was something that took all of an able-bodied man's time."

The same fanatical loyalty that kept Gary's premarital amours from curdling his fans' affection for him governs their reaction to his films. He has been in bad pictures, but to his followers he hasn't been bad in them. They blame everybody else—the director, the producer, the cameraman—never Gary.

Nor is this loyalty restricted to Gary's fans. Jerry Wald, a Hollywood producer, said, "Most actors think they're doing you a favor to work with you. But after the preview of *Task Force*, Cooper came up to me, shook my hand and said, 'Thanks very much.' 'For what?' I wanted to know. 'For a good picture,' he said. I'd never had an actor do that before. Usually they say, 'Don't you think the camera lingered too much on that other fellow?' Thanks is the world's cheapest commodity, but in Hollywood it's mighty rare."

When Bette Davis departed from Warner Brothers, her dressing room was given, not to a stripling wringer of squeals from bobby soxers, but to Gary Cooper.

Gary had never before beefed about the size and shape of his dressing room but the grandeur of the Davis studio diggings so bothered him that he insisted that they be halved before he moved in. This is the only known example of Cooper's being intractable. He has never refused to work with a director, a leading lady or a cameraman. He has never complained about his billing. He has never asked for special favors. In Hollywood these things are even rarer than thanks.   *(1950)*

Not exactly a "Ball of Fire" in the movie of that name, Cooper shows the tight-lipped, taciturn technique that won him Best Actor Oscars for **High Noon** *and* **Sergeant York** *and nominations for three others.*

Beautiful Swede

To some people, unable to see beyond the end of Ingrid Bergman's pert nose or behind the satin curve of her unplucked, unrazored eyebrows, she seems a well-scrubbed, queen-sized woman with a personality that resembles a breeze whipping over a Scandinavian peak. She reminds still others of a lady Channel swimmer minus the usual Channel swimmer's coating of axle grease; or a husky fugitive from a Bryn Mawr basketball squad.

When I met Bergman for our first interview, I mentioned the fact that she had been called normal, wholesome, earthy, sincere, simple, "no sultry siren," "unbeautiful in the Hollywood sense of the word."

She laughed at such plaster-saint labeling. Her laugh is a hearty one that comes from her stomach rather than her lips. She told me that one magazine writer, after visiting her favorite eating places and asking waiters, "Do you know anything bad about Bergman?" and also going to her friends and her co-workers and asking them the same thing, had come to her in desperation to inquire, "Haven't you ever done anything bad? Are you perfect?"

"Of course I've done bad things, but I'm not going to tell you about them," she told him. "That is for you to find out."

Someone prepared a script based upon the life of Sarah Bernhardt for her. But Bernhardt was a tense, artificial redhead with swarms of lovers panting after her and she could do nothing simply. She was thin and little, and Bergman objected, "I'm not the type."

"How many people will know what she was like?" Selznick asked.

"There'll be one who'll know," Bergman said. "Me!"

She is blessed with "bulletproof camera angles," meaning that it is difficult to make her look anything but handsome and at times even beautiful. So far as lighting goes, she is able to work with absolute freedom. Her tallness sometimes requires her to stand in an artificial trench in order not to tower over her shorter leading men. But it is much more important to her than any question of relative height to feel that she knows her co-stars before taking part in an "emotional" screen interlude with them. When her leading man or co-star is a stranger to her, she grows nervous in the big love scenes. Before playing opposite Humphrey Bogart in *Casablanca*, she made repeated efforts to meet him. She visited the studio several times to ask, "Is Mr. Bogart here?"

*The strapping Swede, once described as looking like a Channel swimmer without the axle grease, made her screen debut in European films such as **Munkbrogreven** during the '30s.*

Invariably the answer was "No, he's out on his boat." In desperation, she asked, "Doesn't he ever come for fittings?" Again the answer was no. Obsessed with the thought that she must feel that she knew him, she ran his old films over and over until he was familiar to her.

When it was suggested to her that she send flowers to members of the local press, she refused. "They would feel then that it was an effort on my part to have them say something nice about me in their papers," she objected. "If they like my pictures, that's fine. But if they don't like them, surely they are not so unintelligent as to say they like them just because I have sent them a present."

She can't understand the American custom of endorsing products one doesn't use. She feels that if she really thinks some item is the most wonderful thing of its kind in the world, it might be O.K. to endorse it; otherwise

she would have to be in great need indeed before she'd do such a thing. When she is sent a package of products, she sends it back and tells its sender, "Thank you very much, but if I like your product I'll go out and buy it." Some of those whose merchandise was thus returned grew angry with her and asked irritably, "Just who do you think you are, to come over here and say you don't like our stuff?"

Bergman told me, "In Sweden, my husband was a boxer and swordsman. He loves exercise. In his work as a doctor is much standing still. So now he tries to get his exercise as a gardener around our home, breaking roots and building walls. In Sweden he used to run in the woods with a big rucksack on his back, and I would run with him. Once I said to him, 'I'm hungry. Let's open the rucksack and have lunch.' When he opened it, there were five bricks in it, so that by carrying them he would be stronger. That day we had lunch at a restaurant."

No less than twenty-seven awards—ranging from an Oscar from the Academy of Motion Picture Arts and Sciences to the accolades given her three times by *Box Office* magazine and the New York Drama Critics' Circle—have been showered upon Bergman. It would seem that she must have achieved even her most lofty ambi-

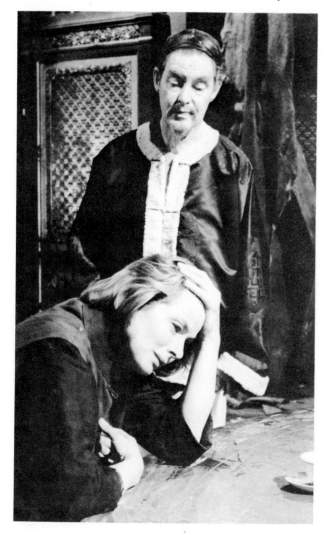

tions. But her most soaring one will not be fulfilled until this fall, when she reaches the screen as Joan of Arc. When Ingrid read about the Maid in school, Joan seemed the biggest part anyone could possibly play. She has never stopped feeling that way about her.

Her solid Broadway success in Maxwell Anderson's play, *Joan of Lorraine,* in 1946 brought her one step nearer her goal and, with Walter Wanger as the guiding spirit behind the enterprise, a Hollywood version of Joan's life was launched. Ironically, her movie portrayal of Joan is so believable, so fully realized that the very excellence of her performance is one of the handicaps under which the picture labors. Those who play smaller roles in the film were carefully selected, but contrasted with the utter sincerity of Bergman's portrayal, they seem—at least in the first few minutes of the picture—merely puppets.

Bergman put endless effort, study and devotion into her characterization of Joan. She spent twenty-two months on research and read nearly 200 books about her. "Almost everybody has tried to use her to put over a message," Bergman told me. "Once they even made her a communist. But we want people to interpret her for themselves."

During the filming of Joan there had been rumors of strife between Victor Fleming and Bergman. It was reported that some of her suggestions had annoyed him.

"She's not superhuman," Fleming told me, when I asked him about it. "She can be stubborn, but her stubbornness is based on an instinct for what makes the best picture." Fleming thought her dead right when, at one point while the picture was being shot, she suggested, "You've got to get me into battle sooner. Up to now, I'm just a girl coming along saying 'Hey, watch out for the British' to the French people."

Joan of Arc was remarkable, but the Swedish girl who will follow a banner sprinkled with lilies across a screen this winter is remarkable too. Perhaps her most remarkable trait of all is her honesty. Hollywood knew that she had turned down a chance to play the Swedish-girl lead in *The Farmer's Daughter,* one of the hits of 1947. But no one had been brash enough to ask her if she had regretted her decision.

"Why don't you go into it while you're having one of your talks with her?" one of her friends urged me.

When I brought it into our conversation, she answered candidly. She admitted that she might have made a mistake in refusing the role. "I could just see myself as a cartoon of a Swede giving a Swedish massage, and I was afraid it would offend the Swedes," she said. "It would not have got me an Academy Award, as it did for Loretta Young. For Loretta, it was new and charming. For me, it would have been just a big Swede playing a big Swede."   *(1948)*

In The Inn of the Sixth Happiness, *Bergman demonstrates the virtuosity that won her three Oscars—for* Gaslight, Anastasia *and* Murder on the Orient Express.

Big John

"Having John Wayne put his arm on your shoulder is like having somebody dump a telephone pole on you."

In picture business some actors lick the handicap of being short by wearing platform shoes or by perching on any empty box while they nuzzle statuesque beauties. Wayne needs no such artificial elevation. He stands six feet four in his socks. His 250 pounds is all lean meat and gristle.

Statistics like these, together with the fact that when he's feeling good at a party he takes on the proportions of a monstrously jovial colossus, may explain why a reference to size seems inevitable in almost any mention of Wayne. More than one critic has written: "Wayne is bigger than the film in which he is appearing." Not long ago a writer implied that he is bigger than the entire motion-picture industry, an estimate based on Wayne's ability to swim upstream against an ebb tide at the box office, carrying a studio or two on his back while doing it.

Even the story of how Wayne got into the movies in the first place requires a reference to his size. The fact that he was a big, hulking kid, rugged enough to play football under Howard Jones at the University of Southern California, brought him to the attention of movie director John Ford.

"At that point everybody in picture business had USC fever," Ford said. "Wayne fell to my lot. I made him a fourth-assistant property man."

The prop man showed signs of becoming something more than that one squally day when Ford was making a submarine picture in the channel that lies between Catalina Island and the California mainland. The script called for stunt men to simulate an escape from the torpedo tubes of a sub helpless on the bottom. They were supposed to dive from the lower deck of the mine sweeper that bore the camera crew, rise to the surface in a bubble of air pumped out beneath the surface, be picked up by rescue boats. It was growing late, the seas were high; the human-porpoise routine was becoming more and more dangerous. Eying the waves smashing against the sweeper's hull, the stunt men balked.

Wayne was busy at his chores on the second deck of the vessel when Ford decided to shame those whose business was selling heroic feats to the movies. He yelled at Wayne, "How about showing these chicken-livered slobs up?"

Without stopping to let go of the pliers and hammer

Wayne plays Sean to Maureen O'Hara's Mary in **The Quiet Man** *(1951). Wayne faced economic ruin from his backing of spectacular flop* **The Alamo,** *which he also directed, but made slow comeback to higher peak than ever.*

he was holding when Ford hailed him, the fourth-assistant prop man hit the waves. His fearlessness so inspired an elderly character actor, who was playing the sub's warrant officer, that he, too, leaped overboard. They repeated it until they were hauled out, blue with cold.

Although Wayne's size got him into pictures, it doesn't keep him out of the private-life altercations that are among the occupational hazard of playing hard-bitten roles. "I'm not a combative-type guy," Wayne said. "I'm a smiling-type guy. But some joker I've never laid eyes on before is always choosing me up for a fight." He detailed a partial list of the pugnacious pests with whom he has to cope:

"Frequently I have to let my hair grow long for a picture. This leads to strangers I meet suggesting that I have characteristics usually associated with long hair,

that are foreign to my nature. I resent these insinuations.

"There is the fellow who comes up to me and asks me to have a cocktail with him. I say that I'm glad to meet him, but that I have to go. His reply is, 'So you're too good to drink with me!', then cocks his fist.

"Then there is the fellow who wants me to come to his table and 'meet my friends.' I've never seen him before, but when I tell him I'll be over as soon as I finish the conversation he's busted in on, he takes it as a personal snub. The result, fireworks."

Wayne does his best to avoid such embroilments. To those who begin their conversations with him by saying, "So you think you're pretty tough, hey?" he replies that he's not nearly so tough as he seems on the screen. "I let them show off before their girls as long as it doesn't make me look too yellow-bellied."

The Big Trail, Wayne's first movie, sank without trace in a flood of red ink. There was a depression on. Theater owners couldn't afford expensive new equipment. The few screens built to accommodate Grandeur Film were so large that 800 buffaloes, rented for one eye-filling sequence, looked like mice when projected upon the vast expanse. The vastness also engulfed the actors' personalities.

Opposite, King of Western stars John Wayne got his big chance in director John Ford's Stagecoach *(1939). After almost four decades of filmmaking, and a long string of classic releases, Wayne was finally awarded his first Oscar in 1969 for* True Grit.

John Wayne was born Marion Michael Morrison in Winterset, Iowa, on May 26, 1907. When he was six, his father moved to California as a homesteader. Shifting to Glendale, the elder Wayne resumed his Iowa occupation of druggist. His son delivered prescriptions busily, but not busily enough to keep him from being an honor student in high school, and, as a result, he won an alternate appointment to Annapolis. Since no dire physical misfortune happened to the boy who had the first call, Wayne never got to the Academy, but he had no trouble matriculating at Southern California.

Raoul Walsh switched his name from Marion Morrison to John Wayne for *The Big Trail*. "I can't have a leading man with a name that sounds like a girl's," Walsh said.   *(1950)*

Wayne played aptly named sailor Duke Slade in the 1937 Pacific potboiler Adventure's End. *Movie also featured Glenn Strange,* Gunsmoke's *bartender and Boris Karloff's successor as monster in* House of Frankenstein.

Sneering Star

When I rang Marlon Brando up, he answered in the slurred, south-of-the-border tones he'd used in the opening sequence of *Viva Zapata!*, not the coarse rumble he'd used in *A Streetcar Named Desire*.

"I can't see you this week," he told me. "My best girl is sick, I must nurse her." The way he said it, it almost sounded "seek," as he would have made it sound in *Viva Zapata!* I got the feeling that I was talking to a Latin who was learning to speak a careful, deliberate English.

"How about next Tuesday?" he suggested.

"When and where?" I asked.

"I will meet you at the studio. We'll go to the beach."

I should have known that he didn't mean what the usual dweller in Hollywood means when he says "to the beach." Preparatory to creeping up on him, I had studied him from afar. My research had indicated that he is a nonconformist and endowed with a genius for the unexpected. He'd brought startled neighbors out of their beds at midnight, their hair spiky, because he'd chosen that hour to pound his African drums. Meeting a movie producer he had made up his mind in advance not to like, he'd held a fresh-laid egg in his hand while the producer shook it vigorously.

Paradoxically—and this makes him even more difficult to pigeonhole—when it comes to sad scenes on the screen, he is a four-handkerchief sentimentalist. Throughout a showing of *The Yearling*, he oozed tears. During a screening of *The Wizard of Oz*, he wept copiously at the touching spots. Not having a handkerchief with him, he'd wiped his tears away on the face of the girl he was dating.

When Marlon first arrived in Hollywood to play the paraplegic veteran in *The Men*, he was still entranced with the rocks-in-the-mouth mumble he'd invented for his part in the stage version of *A Streetcar Named Desire*. *The Men* had started out to be the story of Kenneth Williams, a clean-cut American college boy who'd been injured in World War II. But after half a reel of Brando's repetition of his coal-heaver *Streetcar* delivery, things had to be revised. Kenneth Williams was changed to Ken Wilozek; the name Wilozek was dubbed in where it had been Williams.

Marlon requested that arrangements be made for him to live as a paraplegic patient at Birmingham Veterans' Hospital. He stayed there in a thirty-two-bed ward for four weeks; spent all of his waking hours in a wheelchair. At night, still chair-borne, he accompanied other patients to a nearby cafe. One evening a woman who'd taken one drink too many and was in a crusading mood lectured the wheelchair boys concerning the ability of faith to move mountains. The burden of her preachment was that if they tried hard enough, they could rise from their chairs and

walk. Marlon listened with a show of intense interest. As her exhortations became more fervent, he strained at his chair as if trying to lift himself. Then, with what seemed a superhuman effort, he raised himself to his feet, took two faltering steps, and went into a fast buck and wing. The woman evangelist had to be revived—with water.

I met him in Metro's costume department. A couple of fitters were draping him with one of the togas he was to wear as Marc Antony in *Julius Caesar*. He was clad only in brief purple shorts. They were cut high on each thigh. He had one of those round-muscled bodies which pack more strength than the lumpy ones.

We headed for Santa Monica by way of Venice. Brando announced, "Back East the rocks are gray, dripping things. I don't like the geology there. I haven't yet found a place I'd like to live. Maybe around the Sault Sainte Marie Canal, where they've got big pine trees."

I was to find that he was a great one for taking off on conversational tangents. One moment he'd be talking about one thing; the next, he shifted to another subject. For no reason, he complained that people seldom remembered his name. "They call me Brando Marlo or Marlo Brandon or Mr. Marlon. They seldom get it right.

"You can figure which salary bracket a Hollywood actor is in by the kind of smile he gets," he told me. "When I first came out here I got $40,000 a picture. The smiles people gave me showed two teeth. Now I'm paid around $125,000 a picture. I get both uppers and lowers. But they're locked together. The mouth goes up at the corners. But the teeth are set. I'll never get the big, fat grins that go with $250,000 a picture. They only pay that kind of money to cowboy stars. Each month I'm sent a couple of cowboy scripts, several hunt-and-poke-around-and-chase-'em-in-the-dark movies, and other mongrel literature. I send them back promptly.

"I make a mistake in talking to anybody," Brando said. "What I have to say is either misinterpreted or misunderstood, and I always feel betrayed afterward. But I'm building up armor against this sort of thing," he went on defiantly, "so they can't hurt me anymore." By "they" it was obvious that he meant people like me. He didn't say it with conviction. Nor did it take much insight to see that the bruises left by previous interviewers still hurt.

He did his abrupt conversational shift again. "On the stage you must have a separate characterization for each role," he said. "Hollywood actors don't aspire to that. If a movie actor strikes it rich in one spot, he mines the same

Bare-chested Brando, in Julius Caesar, *1953 (nominated as Best Actor). He used the 1973 Academy presentations as a forum to protest U.S. treatment of native Americans.*

In The Godfather *(1972) Paramount gave Brando the chance to see if he could act with cotton-stuffed cheeks while speaking only in a raspy whisper. He could.*

spot again. And again and again and again and again."

He brooded over that for a while. Then he thought of something he wanted to tell me. "I'm always getting into trouble with those who live by fatuous rules and conventional patterns," he said. "If you challenge their patterns, they resent you. If you tell them, 'What you believe is boring, shallow and childish,' they crucify you."

Brando remarked that he is really the opposite of the young brute he played in *Streetcar*. "I despise that kind of human being," he told me. "I think the reason I was a success in the film version of the play was that during the two years I spent on Broadway in the part, I'd developed a special characterization for it. It is impossible to do this for the usual film. You don't even have time to rehearse properly."

Brando's eyes wandered to a girl. "Some of the most beautiful women in the world are Balinese," he mused.

This made him think of physical fitness. "I take regular exercise because it's an actor's duty to himself to stay healthy and strong," he said. "And I'm a good fencer. I like swimming and country walks. I'm very much a nature man. I rarely go to night spots; only if there's an artist I want to see. My intimates in New York aren't celebrities; they're friends."

I found myself liking him despite the chip he wore on each shoulder. But I was glad I didn't handle his public relations. That way lay stomach ulcers.   *(1953)*

Too much bon vin *resulted in Brando's ebullient but rather inelegant last tangle in Paris as the star is assisted out of a French hotel.*

Public Enemy No.1

People are always saying to me, "Jim, off screen you're a quiet and apparently peaceful guy; yet you've played a lot of hoodlums and other forceful personalities. Have you known people like that in your past? And if you have, does your memory help you with such roles?"

The answer is "Of course."

New York's East Side was full of colorful people while I was growing up. Many had unusual mannerisms of body or speech. I studied them, and from time to time I've used them. Maybe these mannerisms I've collected and have used are one of the reasons that, along with Jimmy Stewart, Clark Gable and Cary Grant, I seem to be a target for mimics. Most impersonators think they are taking me off when what they're really doing is imitating me imitating a character I knew back in the neighborhood where I grew up.

George Kelly's 1929 play, *Maggie the Magnificent*, was the turning point in my life. *Maggie* didn't last very long, but it lasted long enough. Because I was seen in it, I was hired for a play called *Penny Arcade*, opposite Joan Blondell, and Warner Brothers bought the play and made it into a film. They not only bought·it, they hired me at $500 a week with a three-week guarantee plus my train fare to the coast. After that Warners put me into *Doorway to Hell*, with Lew Ayers, and my wife came West to be with me.

My part in *Doorway* was "next to lead." I was the pal of the big gangster, a big underworld heavy. The script called for me to be a light-comedy hoodlum; I had some fly lines to say—meaning flip and quick. A part in a film called *Public Enemy* was next suggested to me. I said, "Fine." I didn't even read the script. If anybody blew a whistle and said, "Act!" I acted. I was a contract player in the Warners' stock company, and a studio contract player is not choosy about parts. Anyhow, once the show-business ball starts bouncing, you don't make plans. You think you are dribbling it down the floor, but you're only watching it bounce.

Two fellows, Kubec Glasmon and John Bright, had written *Beer and Blood*, a story of two young Chicago hoods who were making their presence felt with guns and beer-running during the prohibition era in Chicago. That was the basis of the film called *Public Enemy*. Warner had borrowed a good actor, Eddie Woods, from First National, to play the lead, and I was set to play the second lead. Then Glasmon and Bright saw *Doorway to Hell* and said to the Warner management, "You'd better switch the two parts around." Bill Wellman, who was to direct, also held

As a shoot-'em-up gangster, Cagney stole two Best Actor nominations, but it took a singing and tap-dancing **Yankee Doodle Dandy** *to win the big one.*

that view. They told me later that what they saw in me was a "street-gamin quality and a brashness" which they thought right for the part. They went to Darryl Zanuck, who was then head of production at Warner Brothers, and the switch was made.

Mae Clarke played "moll" to my "gangster." The thing that the public remembers about *Public Enemy* is the scene in which I shoved half a grapefruit into Mae's face. That half grapefruit has become a piece of Americana. It was just about the first time, if not the very first, that a woman had been treated like a broad on the screen, instead of like a delicate flower.

That bit of business became so identified with me that years afterward, when I'd go into a restaurant, people would send me half grapefruits with their compliments, and I got so tired of that deal I began to duck eating in public. *(1956)*

Bogie Man
by Cameron Shipp

Humphrey de Forest Bogart is a whisky-drinking actor who has been hooting at Hollywood and making fun of its pretensions for twenty-two years.

This year he won the Motion Picture Academy of Arts and Sciences' Oscar, a seven-pound, gold-plated, sixty-four-dollar statuette, Hollywood's highest gift, which is meant to prove that the recipient is the best actor in the world. When the Oscar was thrust at him, Bogart shuddered with amazement, foozled his ad-lib, and muttered something polite. He recovered from this slip in a matter of seconds, however, and proclaimed to the press that it was all bunk, that the only true test of ability would be to have all the silly actors don black tights and recite *Hamlet*.

This calculated insult pleased him, but Bogart itched with shame over his earlier slip until next morning, when his son Steve, a sturdy three-year-old, restored family honor and dismissed all nonsense by seizing the Oscar and hurling it at his parent. One day last year, John Huston, the director, called Bogie on the telephone.

"I have a great story," Huston said. "The hero is a low-life. You are the biggest low-life in town and therefore suitable for the part."

Enchanted by this approach, Bogart suggested that the two of them drink lunch. The upshot of the encounter was that they hurried over to call on Katharine Hepburn and reveal to her the enticements of a story about a skinny missionary spinster and a gin-swizzling clown floating down an incredible African river to fire a homemade torpedo at a German gunboat.

This strange tale, written by C. S. Forester and published in 1935, had been despaired of by every studio in town, but Huston, Hepburn and Bogart saw the fun and sentiment in it, deferred their salaries in order to have cash to make it, and went all the way to Africa to shoot it.

By all accounts, the boys treated Miss Hepburn like dirt, a reverse twist for this distinguished actress which, apparently, she liked enormously. She lectured them sharply about whisky drinking, without which both Huston and Bogart found Africa unendurable, but responded happily when Bogart gave his usual command: "Ah, get yourself a chair, Katie, and pull one up for me. And fix the drinks."

The African safari was rugged in every respect, but only two incidents linger in Bogart's memory. Once the party ran out of Scotch for two days and naturally descended to the nadir of despair, and once they were attacked by ants, which bit everybody. But Bogart has had it tough before, will make at least a quarter of a million dollars from a venture everyone thought was downright absurd, and is inclined to lump his good picture and his Oscar as just another one of those things.

Whether Humphrey Bogart could possibly be as tough as he acts in pictures is a matter frequently in dispute.

Richard Brooks, writer-producer-director pal, recalls the time Bogart met a genuine Free French underground fighter at a party.

Wife Lauren Bacall said he was "truly a gentle soul, rather old-fashioned." He brought a new dimension to tough guy roles by invoking audience sympathy.

Sam, Rick and Ilsa, taking the sting out of Nazi occupation. Sam (Dooley Wilson) could sing, act and drum, but his piano-playing had to be dubbed into Casablanca.

"Do something tough," said the underground man, acknowledging the introduction.

"You got the wrong guy," said Bogart.

"I can eat glass," said the Frenchman. He did. He chewed and swallowed a champagne glass. Bogart expressed admiration.

"I can also eat razor blades," said the Frenchman. He proceeded to do so. "Well," he urged, "if you can't do that, let's mix some drinks."

The Frenchman then mixed vermouth, gin, Scotch, bourbon, *crème de cacao*, champagne and brandy. On home grounds now, Bogart thirstily matched the tough man. Stayed right with him. No chaser.

"I still don't think you're tough," said the Frenchman. "You can't eat glass."

"Oh, I can so," said Bogart. He grabbed a cocktail glass, snapped it, chewed it and tried to swallow. Nothing went down, but blood gushed copiously from his cut mouth and lips.

"I guess you are all right," said the Frenchman. "We are both very tough guys. Let us go now and insult women together."

Dave Chasen, who throws Bogie out of his restaurant once or twice a month for old times' sake, is the author of two sentences which come close to summing the man up.

"He's a hell of a guy until eleven-thirty," says Dave.

"The only trouble is, he thinks he's Bogart."   *(1952)*

Son of a rich New York doctor, Bogart had a pitted-stone, urban façade, but there was a streak of sentiment as long and flashy as a gangster's funeral.

Great Scott
by Bill Davidson

One day in November, 1958, actor George C. Scott awoke in a New York City jail. He was then appearing in his first Broadway play, *Comes a Day*, but the police failed to recognize him when they took him in for arraignment.

"It was like a nightmare," Scott recalls. "They grabbed me and snapped handcuffs on my wrists and said I should be a nice boy and not get violent. I went to court, stood manacled before the judge and learned that while I had been drunk the previous evening, I had beaten up a man at a party. I was charged with felonious assault. I realized then I had fallen into an abyss of alcoholism from which I *had* to pull myself out."

Today, five years after the incident, Scott not only has

pulled himself out, but has established himself as one of the finest actors in the world. He has earned Academy Award nominations for his work in the movies *The Hustler* and *Anatomy of a Murder* and drawn raves for his performances on the stage in Shakespeare. This season he has won acclaim as star of his own successful CBS-TV series, "East Side, West Side" in which he plays a social worker.

The frustrations began to pile on young Scott at an early age. After an uneventful four years at high school in the Detroit suburbs, he enlisted in the Marine Corps and was stationed in Washington, D.C.

When his enlistment ended in 1949, he entered the University of Missouri School of Journalism. "The deeper I got into journalism," he says, "the more I realized I wasn't right for it. I was terribly embarrassed about asking questions of other people." In his confusion, Scott eventually tried out for a college play, *The Winslow Boy*. He got a part and then performed in five more plays. "That did it," says Scott. "I was hooked."

While a student at the university, Scott also acted in a theatrical company at nearby Stephens College for women. Just before he was scheduled to graduate in 1952, he fell in love with Carolyn Hughes, a Stephens girl in the acting group, and they decided to get married. Scott recalls, "I got jobs acting in stock companies in Toledo and Detroit. We were living hand-to-mouth and then, when a baby came, it got worse. So did my drinking. Carolyn and I separated in 1953, and she got a divorce in 1954."

"Later," says Scott, "I got a part in a Pirandello play, married another actress, Pat Reed, and the struggle started all over again . . . my drinking got worse. The more successful I got, the worse the drinking became."

Then Scott's second marriage shattered. But brilliant even when sodden, he continued to grow as an actor. He did Shakespeare's *As You Like It* and then *Children of Darkness*. His co-star in *Children of Darkness* was the fiery actress, Colleen Dewhurst, who became his third wife.

His life with Colleen and their sons, Alexander, two, and Campbell, one, has been almost idyllic. Despite the fact that his rampant idealism has led him into a tangled financial web, Scott seems almost unreasonably buoyant nowadays.   *(1963)*

Scott was nominated three times for an Academy Award, but George C.'s Oscar (for his appearance in Patton*) rests unclaimed in the Academy vault. He announced in advance of the ceremonies that he would refuse to accept it.*

Raft on Trial

If you suspect that I know a great deal about gangsters and their world, you are right. If you think I made mistakes in my foolish youth, you are also right. But you are wrong if you believe that I have ever deliberately hurt anyone. If I were to be called before a grand jury today—and this is one experience I've never had—the examination might go like this:

Q.: Your real name is George Raft?

A.: No. My name was Ranft but I dropped the "n" because Raft was easier to pronounce. My father never forgave me for that.

Q.: Have you ever been arrested or tried or convicted for a crime?

A.: Never. But perhaps I should have been. When I used to visit Owney Madden in Sing Sing he was always ribbing me. "When they bring you in here someday," he would say, "I'll get you a low number."

Q.: Did you ever pick pockets or roll a drunk?

A.: Yes, I'm sorry to say. During prohibition we thought all the customers in the speakeasies were fair game.

Q.: Have you ever killed a man?

A.: No. I came close several times, and I thank God for staying my hand. When I was a kid in the Hell's Kitchen district you had to fight for your life every day. I had a terrible temper in earlier years.

Q.: Isn't it true that the underworld got you into the movies?

A.: Not exactly. The underworld put up money so I could try my luck in Hollywood. I flopped the first time and they gave me enough so I could make a second trip West.

Q.: Isn't it a fact, Mr. Raft, that you were an intimate friend of Al Capone, Buggsy Siegel——

A.: Excuse me. It's Benny Siegel. He hated to be called Buggsy, and nobody in the mob dared use that word. Joe Adonis, Lucky Luciano, Mickey Cohen and Frank Costello. Yes, I knew them. They were all friends of mine.

Q.: And what did you get out of all this, Mr. Raft?

A.: Gentlemen, I am the loneliest man in Hollywood.

There comes a time in every man's life when his account is overdrawn and he has to balance the books. So this is for Jackie Dietz, who said I was a gangster. And for any others who have George Raft on their ledger as a no-good so-and-so who earned $10 million as a movie villain—not because he was a great actor, but only because he was doing what comes naturally.

He hosted "George Raft's Colony Club"—then London's most successful gambling casino—until 1967, when he was barred from England as an undesirable alien.

It is also for my mother, who thought it was quite wonderful that her first-born son, Georgie, the only one of her six children who lived, remained a movie star and miraculously stayed out of jail at the same time.

I am sure she was never quite convinced I had any virtues, but toward the end of her life she came over to my side, right or wrong. Shortly before her death in 1937 I took her to a premiere in New York, and the studio, as usual, provided me with a police escort. As we entered the lobby, trailed by four husky, uniformed patrolmen, she suddenly became aware of them.

"Run, Georgie, run!" she screamed, giving me a push. "Don't let the cops get you!"

So I say again that this is for my sweet mother—wherever she may be—and to assure her that the cops didn't get me, but that my conscience did. A man can't run forever. *(1957)*

Frame-up
by Frederick C. Othman

Edward G. Robinson bought his first painting at an auction for two dollars. That was in 1913, after he had studied law at Columbia and had landed his first job on the stage. It was a bad rendition of a fat cow, but she had a warm-looking, chocolate-colored coat, and Robinson liked to look at her. "I never thought, when I bought her, that life would come to this," he said. "I love my paintings. I have spent more for them than I can afford."

Although he was a successful stage actor, he never could afford to indulge his tastes in art until the movies took him over and made of him one of the toughest, meanest gangsters ever to slap his moll with the wrong end of an automatic. Eventually, one movie after another

began to end with Robinson sizzling in the electric chair to prove that crime does not pay. For each sizzle he received a reported $100,000, and then he was off on a tour as a patron of the arts. As his collection grew, other collectors charged that it was something dreamed up by his press agents. If space in the papers were what he wanted, he believes he could think of less expensive ways of getting it than buying Renoirs. "The result would be better and the cost less," he insisted, "if I collected race horses, pink elephants or even wives."

When the Depression was at its depth, a woman in Philadelphia announced that she was getting rid of her collection. Robinson called, took plenty of time to look at her pictures and bought a Pissarro, a Degas and a Monet. "They appealed to my emotions," he said. "They weren't intellectual picture puzzles. I liked them all. Gladys liked them, too, and since the price was very reasonable, she didn't kick. That's what really got me started. It was fun buying those pictures and more fun owning them."

He'd bought several American pictures by now, including Grant Wood's *Daughters of the Revolution*. This was the portrait of three dour women which had been exhibited almost everywhere, with a constant crowd in front of it. Robinson saw it in New York, noticed in the catalogue that it was on loan from a dealer, and rushed over to see him. To the Last Gangster's amazement, they came to terms in ten minutes. "Apparently nobody else even thought of the possibility that such a celebrated painting could be for sale," he said. "When I bought it, they started kicking themselves."

He'd hardly brought the picture home before his wife gave a tea and discovered, too late, that she had seated the state regent of the D. A. R. directly under it. "It was my most embarrassing experience," she says, "except one. That was when we lent this same picture to the Museum of Modern Art and we went to look at it, and Eddie thought he saw some dirt on it. He subscribes to the theory that the best cleanser for bringing out the color of oil paintings is saliva on a handkerchief. So he spit on his handkerchief and went to work scrubbing this painting, and the guard came up and said, 'Hey, mister, you can't do that.' Eddie swung around, and he looked like a gangster for real, and he said, 'What do you mean, I can't do that?' " *(1944)*

Never nominated for an Oscar, "Little Caesar" appeared in 101 films. Given a special Oscar for his contributions to the industry in 1973, he was not alive to receive the award.

The Role
I Liked Best...

The Role I Liked Best was a popular *Post* back-of-the-book feature from 1945 to 1955. In that ten-year period, more than 300 stars told the readers of the *Post* about their triumphs (for the most part) on the silver screen. Whether noble, ignoble, funny or sad, the reasons for their selections were never dull.

by Sidney Greenstreet

Usually a movie-villain role has to be played in a monotone because the menace is written in one key, emphasizing a single personal quality. In contrast, Dashiell Hammett's Kasper Gutman, the Fat Man, of *The Maltese Falcon*, is a colorful, stimulating character and, happily, John Huston kept close to the novel in making his fine adaptation. I enjoyed the way the character became progressively more interesting with each scene—did not lose its appeal beyond a certain point, as roles sometimes do.

The cameramen helped me achiéve the effect of fatness. To be sure, I'm not exactly a flyweight; I weighed 285 pounds at the time. But by bringing the camera near the floor and shooting up, they made me weigh about 350.

The Maltese Falcon was my first picture. The studios had suggested several times that I leave the stage, but I was busy and happy with the Lynn Fontanne and Alfred Lunt company. When Warners' offered me the Gutman role, I wasn't confident about doing it on the screen, agreeing to try it only when the studio assured me they were willing to take the chance.

Contributing to the pleasure of my favorite role was the exceptionally able cast—Humphrey Bogart, Mary Astor, Peter Lorre, Ford Bond and the others—and our discovery that John Huston, who was making his first directorial effort, was a natural at that type of work, which isn't the case with everyone who tries it. John senses the drive of a story and knows how to keep it alive. An example of how cooperative everybody in the cast was came up when Humphrey Bogart missed some lines and I, forgetting I was not on the stage, but in the presence of sound equipment which picks up and magnifies even a whisper, softly prompted him. But Humphrey, a stage veteran himself, took my strange behavior sympathetically in stride as we went back and did the scene all over again.

(Above) When Greenstreet played a "heavy," as was the case more often than not, he gave double meaning to the word. (Below) Spotting Hitchcock's brief appearances is a favorite pastime of movie buffs.

The Role I Liked Best . . .

By ALFRED HITCHCOCK

MANY movie-goers think I play bit parts in the films I direct as a good-luck gesture that insures their success. That's nonsense. I've had my share of flops. Actually, I started putting myself in pictures twenty-five years ago in order to save the cost of extra players. I continued it from habit, I guess, or maybe because I'm just a frustrated ham.

My favorite role was in the picture Lifeboat, and I had an awful time thinking it up. Usually I play a passer-by, but you can't have a passer-by out on the ocean. I thought of being a dead body floating past the lifeboat, but I was afraid I'd sink. And I couldn't play one of the nine survivors, as each had to be played by a competent actor or actress.

Finally I hit on the perfect plan. I was on a strenuous diet at the time, working my way painfully down from 300 to 200 pounds. So I decided to immortalize my reduction and get my bit part by posing for "before" and "after" pictures. These photographs were used in a newspaper advertisement of an imaginary drug, Reduco, and the audience saw them—and me—when William Bendix opened an old newspaper he had picked up on the boat.

This role was a great hit. Letters literally poured in from fat people, asking where they could buy Reduco, the miracle drug that had helped me lose 100 pounds. Maybe I shouldn't admit it, but I got a certain satisfaction from writing back that the drug didn't exist, and adding smugly that the best way to lose weight was to go on a strenuous diet, as I had done.

The Role I Liked Best . . .

BY ERROL FLYNN

IMAGINATIVE stories always have attracted me far more than realistic ones. That's why Robin Hood is my favorite role.

It was pure fairy tale, yet through weeks of careful training we made it realistic in detail.

Robin Hood, naturally, had to be expert with the bow and arrow. To achieve the appearance of genuine skill, I was coached by the world-famous archer, Howard Hill, who taught me how to be quick on the draw, from quiver to bow, and how to make the arrows hit their mark. Hill appeared in the film as captain of the archers and had to shoot a man in an important scene. To make this realistic, the studio put a pad in the armor of the man who acted as the target. Hill hit the center of the pad with just enough force to make the arrow stick. If he had

missed the pad or shot too hard, we would have lost a stunt man.

Another expert, Fred Cavens, taught me how to use the broadsword. I also had to master, more or less, the use of the quarterstaff in order to fight with Little John on a log bridge. We both fell into the stream at the end of this contest, a touch I liked very much.

Michael Curtiz is a fine director, but, in his search for perfection, he pulled a very fast one on me. This was while we were shooting the scene where Robin Hood brings in a deer and flings it on a table. Robin Hood was supposed to be dead tired, and I tried to look that way, but Curtiz wasn't satisfied. He made me repeat the scene about 699 times. By that time, I was dead tired, and Curtiz was satisfied.

Lorre began his cinematic career as a child molester in the German film, M, *working his way up from pervert to the sniveling hood in* The Maltese Falcon.

by Peter Lorre

Usually there is no future in murder. But in Hollywood, where the unusual is encountered constantly, cinematic violence can be made to pay a pretty penny. My favorite set of movie misdeeds came in connection with the role of Raskolnikov in the picture *Crime and Punishment*.

I liked the role because it was one of the most tragic of all time, and because it was part of one of the greatest classics in literature. It was a stark, honest part and, happily, most of its honesty was preserved in the film. Not a single extra was used in the picture, because director Josef von Sternberg wanted to eliminate everything that might possibly distract the audience from the story itself.

My first job in connection with this role was to persuade the studio to produce *Crime and Punishment*. I realized the book was too long for the studio head to read, but I also knew that no intelligent person would attempt to make a short synopsis of this great novel. So I hit on the idea of getting a not-so-intelligent secretary to jump in where intellectual angels might fear to tread, and she turned out a fine two-page synopsis.

The studio head read it and thought the story was wonderful. In fact, he is reported to have said, "A book like that ought to get published!"

by Fredric March

I was a reluctant conscript to the role that became my favorite. When Samuel Goldwyn sent me MacKinlay Kantor's book, on which the picture was based, I thought it interesting but extremely long. Later, when Goldwyn phoned to ask if I would take the part of Al Stephenson, I hesitated because I was anxious to see the finished script before making a decision. Finally Goldwyn told me that Robert Sherwood was doing the script, and that Myrna Loy, Dana Andrews, Teresa Wright and Harold Russell, the armless veteran, would be in the cast.

To say that I capitulated after all this makes me sound like a city that had been under siege, and suggests an importance I don't deserve. Actually, I was just feeling around for a good part, and that's what I got. The role of Al Stephenson in *The Best Years of Our Lives* was an honest role in a fine picture. It dramatized the problems of the returning veteran in a down-to-earth way—at a time when servicemen were coming back by the thousands.

I especially enjoyed working with Harold Russell, a naturally fine actor with a grand sense of humor. The part of Al Stephenson showed how veterans' problems could be handled with humane understanding; and this gave me the feeling that I had made a tiny contribution toward the solution of one of our biggest postwar tasks.

(Above) Errol buckled a few swashes off camera also, hence the origin of the phrase "in like Flynn." (Below) Being two-faced won March in first Oscar for Dr. Jekyll and Mr. Hyde. He won his second for his favorite role.

Minstrels, Jesters & Ghosts

Sound Idea

by Al Jolson

The Jazz Singer appealed to me more than any other role because it was a story of my own experiences. I was reliving part of my life—my early environment and bringing up, my refusal to follow in my father's footsteps and become a rabbi, my unbreakable preoccupation with singing and acting.

When I was in Champaign, Illinois, Samson Raphaelson showed me a short story he had written, "The Day of Atonement." And as I started making the picture, in 1927, I was thrilled by the fact that it was to be the first picture to have singing in it, but I didn't dream it would also introduce dialogue to the screen. The speaking was accidental. When I sat down to the piano as we began work on a singing scene, I ad libbed, "Wait till you hear this, mamma! If I'm a big hit, I'm going to take you to Coney Island and I'll buy you a black silk dress that'll make a noise when you walk!" Warners decided the words might be effective; several takes were made—and the moving pictures had begun to talk.

After the picture was released, Lee Shubert and I used to go every night to the theater just to watch the scene in which I sang the "Kol Nidre." I try not to take successes or failures to heart, but *The Jazz Singer* captured and still holds a favorite place in my memories. *(1946)*

The jazz singer with pretty boys Dick Powell and Rudy Vallee. The year 1977 marked a half century of talkies.

Who Loves Judy Garland?

by Cameron Shipp

It begins invariably with professions of love and esteem. It takes various forms, but the gist is this: "She's the greatest, that girl. Got the most exciting talent in show business. Who else can belt over a song like Judy Garland? She's the greatest, that's all. I tell you, I love her, but——"

A dirge follows. The dirge says, sometimes with flat statements and claims to inside knowledge, sometimes with studious hints, that Judy is washed up, kaputt, through, and will never work again.

This statement is becoming so familiar in Hollywood that it is almost classic. Judy has been consigned to oblivion more often than any other actress. By now, her farewell performances probably exceed Sarah Bernhardt's memorable and frequent good-byes. Actually, Hollywood is not being merely smug and cruel about this. On the record, Judy Garland has accommodated the gossips many times by falling on her face, breaking contracts, walking out on pictures, and by collapsing in hospitals under the care of psychiatrists. She does things like this after almost every success. Five years ago she went the limit with a highly publicized but fortunately inept attempt to cut her throat.

On the whole, Judy has made the happiest and most tuneful pictures—more of this kind by far than any other star in Hollywood save perhaps Bing Crosby. But she has been Hollywood's unhappiest star. Roger Edens, who wrote many of her great song hits, puts it like this: "She ought to enjoy being the enormous international celebrity she is. But she doesn't enjoy it. She doesn't know it. She has more talent than anybody who ever came along, but she doesn't understand that either. Everybody loves Judy, but she thinks nobody loves her."

She grew up, literally, before the eyes of millions of spectators. She became a major star with *Broadway Melody*, when she was barely fifteen. *Love Finds Andy Hardy*, *The Wizard of Oz* and *Strike Up the Band* came soon after, and Judy became an international institution—

Judy and Buddy Ebsen (television's Jed Clampett and Barnaby Jones) in M-G-M's Broadway Melody of 1938. *Judy played the child-star daughter of Sophie Tucker in the movie, sang "Dear Mr. Gable," which she had sung earlier at the studio party for Clark's 36th birthday.*

everybody's little girl.

When Judy was fourteen she was overworked. She made twelve big pictures in her teens. She was harassed by demands that she dance, cry and act before the cameras, as well as do the one thing she knew she could do—sing. She stuffed herself with all the food she could cram at every meal, sneaked in double malts between scenes, and swelled unphotogenically fat. An M-G-M executive sent for her.

"You look like a hunchback," he told her. "We love

you, but you're so fat you look like a monster."

The child tried to twinkle through her tears, then ran. Old-timers who told me this incident still regard it as the most brutal pronouncement ever made in Hollywood to a small girl. Judy tells the story today with a smile, but you can see that it still hurts. At the time she was called a monster she was violently in love with Clark Gable.

From the beginning, Judy's pictures were big, requiring long, wearying rehearsals and recording stints.

She often speaks wistfully of M-G-M, in the fond way a person may speak of a stern parent, but when the subject gets around to reducing, Judy's big eyes snap with sheer hatred. Hedda Hopper tells me she once saw Judy trying to do a dance sequence and almost dropping from exhaustion.

"I'm too hungry," she told her director.

"Get on with it," the director said. "Get on with it and you won't feel hungry."

Long hours and starvation exhausted her, and then

Judy Garland, young, was a healthy, mature woman. Old, she became the waif of filmdom: desperate, ill, thin in voice and purse. Drugs and the adulation of her fans kept her afloat until age 47. Annual TV showings of The Wizard of Oz *serve as a tribute to and reminder of the star's talent.*

insomnia set in. Judy found an instant and easy solution for that problem: she took pills. The next step was pills to wake her up. She became a virtual automaton, turned off and on by formulas.

In the interests of this story, I scraped acquaintance with a psychiatrist who treated Judy Garland a few years ago. I asked him, "Why does Judy Garland run, why does she walk out of productions, why does she collapse and hide under beds, so to speak?"

"Why, that's easy enough," the doctor said. "Everybody wants to creep under beds and hide from the bad old world. I want to. You want to. But if you or I did it, some member of the family would come along and say, 'Hey, boy, get out from under there and stop making a fool of yourself.' And we would come out, be ashamed and behave.

"But when a movie star crawls under a bed a battery of eight hairdressers, six secretaries and a flock of psychiatrists gather around and murmur, 'Oh, you poor dear.' So the star gets what you'd probably call a conditioned reflex and crawls under the nearest bed the next time she is miffed. Tell me, now, how are you feeling? How is your mental health after talking to movie people day after day?"   *(1955)*

Hollywood's Fabulous Brat

by Stanley Frank

Early in 1940 Mickey Rooney was elected by audiences and exhibitors the box-office champion of 1939—a distinction he was to hold for three successive and unprecedented years. He was nineteen years old and already recognized as the most facile and versatile performer in the movies. He was alternating between the enormously successful Hardy comedies and elaborate musicals with Judy Garland in which he sang, danced, played the piano and drums and gave impersonations.He was the most valuable property in the industry—and he was earning $750 a week, less than any supporting player on the MGM payroll.

Then, as now, Rooney was five feet, one and a half inches tall, he had a face not unlike a shriveled grapefruit and he was driven by an almost pathological impatience to grow up, physically and professionally. He had nothing to offer but sheer talent, and he was selling it so well before he was two years old that people thought he was a midget. Born with an adult aplomb and a set of baritone vocal cords that leapfrogged childhood and adolescence, he was the star of the Mickey McGuire comedies at six and, seventy-eight pictures later, was washed up at twelve. Considered the least promising youngster in Hollywood because of his wizened, old-before-his-time appearance, he outclawed and outacted competition for choice juvenile roles in the next two years.

The public shortly will see more tangible evidence of Rooney's maturity in his next picture, *Killer McCoy*. Playing an adult role for the first time in his career, Rooney is cast as a tough, ruthless prize fighter with a *cum laude* degree from poolrooms and a Ph.D. in gutter lore.

"I'll never make another Hardy picture," Mickey says. "I'm fed up with those dopey, insipid parts. How long can a guy play a jerk kid? I'm twenty-seven years old. I've been divorced once and separated from my second wife. I have two boys of my own. I spent almost two years in the Army. It's time Judge Hardy went out and bought me a double-breasted suit. With long pants. I'm tired of musicals, too, although I would like to do *Finian's Rainbow*, the Broadway hit. The part of the leprechaun could've been written for me. It's perfect for me.

Rooney's feet and face made his fortune. The superb dancer's enthusiasm made hackneyed plots new again.

"What sort of pictures do I want to make? Straight dramatic stuff where you have a chance to act. They say I've got to play juveniles on account of my size until I drop dead from hardening of the arteries. After *Killer McCoy* is released, I'll never have to worry about another role. All right, I'm not going to grow taller and I'll never look like Robert Taylor, but I can play the parts that made James Cagney and Edward G. Robinson famous. They're not much bigger than I am. People think I'm touchy about my

Lewis Stone and Mickey in Judge Hardy and Son, *seventh in the fifteen-picture series that made Rooney a star.*

height, but, honest, it's the last thing that enters my mind. If I was a six-foot pretty boy, the chances are I wouldn't have half my ability and fire. There are advantages in being small. It's easier to get lost in a crowd."

That last observation will provoke raucous laughter in Hollywood, where Rooney is considered the most tireless exhibitionist of a community which does not brand celebrities as eccentric until they hang by the toes from chandeliers in public places.

"People look at me and say, 'There's a lucky bum who got all the breaks,' " Rooney flares. "Nuts. Did anybody help me when I beat out two hundred and seventy-five kids for the McGuire part? When my mom and I didn't have what to eat, I made a screen test for Paramount. It's still on the shelf. I played second fiddle at MGM to Freddie Bartholomew and Jackie Cooper for four, five years. Where are they today? I was the biggest money-maker in the joint, and I was getting a lousy seven-fifty a week. Yeah, I got the breaks—all in the neck."

Recently, on the simultaneous celebration of his twenty-seventh birthday and twenty-fifth anniversary in show business, Mickey was bawled out by his mother for coddling his sons, Mickey, Jr., two, and Timothy, ten months old. His mother upbraided him for failing to use his influence to put the children into the movies.

"I'm not going to repeat mistakes made with me," he answered. "My kids will have normal childhoods. They won't go to work until they're four or five."   *(1947)*

Rooney was the number-one box office star in 1939, '40 and '41, enlisted after filming of National Velvet *and served in the Army for two years.*

Dueling
Dance Shoes
by Pete Martin

A few years ago, when Hollywood heard that Astaire and Kelly, the movies' two ace dancers, were to be teamed together in a movie version of the *Ziegfeld Follies*, it pricked up its ears for the crackle of onstage lightning. Says Arthur Freed, who produced the picture, "A lot of sadistic characters who hoped to witness a fight to a finish with tap shoes as weapons were disappointed. Instead of infighting and gouging in the clinches, Fred and Gene staged an Alphonse and Gaston act. They threw themselves into it with so much abandon that it became fascinating to see how far they'd go. A long time before we decided to make the picture, Astaire had told me, 'This Kelly is good. I don't usually like dancers, but he gives me a kick.' And Gene had sought me out to say, 'Fred has been my idol ever since I put on dancing shoes. Fifty years from now, when they show old films, he'll be the dancer they'll pick to represent his era.' "

Freed says that there'd been a lot of amiable bickering around town as to which of the two was the better dancer, and that it seemed a hot idea to toss them both into the same dance number and let people make their own decision. He started the ball rolling by telling Gene, "I'd like to do a number with you and Fred in it." "That's fine," Gene said. "Any dance Fred would like to do, I'll do." Then Freed talked to Fred, who agreed, "It's a swell idea. What does Gene want to?" Freed suggested a number called "The Babbitt and the Bromide," that Fred had once done.

"I put them together in a rehearsal hall and left them alone," Freed says. "At the end of the day, Kelly came to me and said, 'I can't see what Fred sees in this Babbitt-Bromide routine. I think we'd be better off doing an Indian number.' Like any two champions they naturally wanted to do the thing they could do best, but their respect for each other was so great that they were extremely polite when they were working together, and if they had any suggestions, they made them to me. Somehow, Fred discovered that Gene was unhappy about "The Babbitt and the Bromide," and he came to me and said that

perhaps they ought to do the Indian number after all. After that it became a kind of contest in politeness, for when Gene heard that Fred wanted him to have his way, he did a switch and began to insist upon doing "The Babbitt and the Bromide." Gene's Alphonse finally outbowed Fred's Gaston, and both poured it on so beautifully in "The Babbitt and the Bromide" that folk who collect big moments in the movies the way other people collect old masters rank it well up their lists.   *(1950)*

Debbie Reynolds and Gene Kelly in Singing in the Rain.
Kelly started out to be a lawyer, left Ripon College in Wisconsin to start his own dancing schools, later combined Broadway techniques with classic steps in Hollywood.

He's Entertainment

It is difficult for me to decide why I liked the role of Jerry Travers in *Top Hat* better than any other. I guess it was because Jerry was a buoyant, carefree person with a nice sense of humor. The picture itself was one of the best Ginger Rogers and I ever did together, and it was the first I ever made with Irving Berlin's music, which helped a lot.

In a way, *Top Hat* marked a milestone in screen musical comedies. Nearly all the other screen musicals had dealt with the backstage problems of their characters. But in *Top Hat* I played the part of a successful professional dancer whose problems of love and romance came entirely from his private life.

The idea for the dance number which finally gave the picture its name came to me in the middle of the night. I woke suddenly, visualizing a row of top-hatted men. I saw myself shooting them down, one by one, with my walking stick, while I simulated the sound of a machine gun with my tapping feet. I was so stirred by the possibilities of this number that I jumped out of bed, grabbed a handy umbrella and started practicing it. Soon my sister, Adele, called from the next room of our apartment to ask what in the world I was doing.

"Oh, nothing," I said. "I just had an idea for a number."

"Well," Adele said coldly, "this perhaps isn't the best time of the day to try it out."

That comment ended my practice session. But the dance idea persisted, and finally took its place with other numbers in the picture, like "Cheek to Cheek" and "Isn't It a Lovely Day To Be Caught in the Rain."   *(1948)*

Astaire and Ginger Rogers (below) dance "Cheek to Cheek" in Top Hat*; they made eleven movies together. (Right) Fred with Eleanor Powell and future senator George Murphy, who began dancing after a mining injury.*

A Hard Day's Night

by Alfred G. Aronowitz

When the Beatles stepped from the plane, 1,500 people shrieked a welcome from the roof of Liverpool Airport. This was only the vanguard of the 150,000 who lined the 10-mile route to the town hall. On the drive to the city the Beatles had an eight-motorcycle escort. The mobs kept breaking through the police lines to claw at their car, while the police motorcycles raced down both gutters, making spectators jump hotfootedly back onto the curbs. Along the way the motorcycle police heard radio reports that there was rioting at town hall.

The Beatles—Ringo Starr, John Lennon, Paul McCartney, George Harrison—were home. They were back in Liverpool for the opening of their first movie, *A Hard Day's Night.*

At the Liverpool town hall the first of the 400 persons hurt that day were being carried on stretchers from the crowds surging and screaming behind the barricades. The Beatles were rushed into the office of the Lord Mayor, a small moustached man named Louis Caplan. He was wearing white tie and tails and something called the Lord Mayor's evening jewel, a cameo which hung from his neck by a blue ribbon and was decorated by the Liverpool coat of arms surrounded by diamonds, emeralds and rubies. The first thing that John did was to press his nose against the jewel. "All right," said the Lord Mayor as he waved an envelope bearing a British Columbia postmark. "Now, John. Which one of you is John? There's a letter here for you from Victoria."

"Queen Victoria?" asked John.

"All right," said the Lord Mayor, "now Ringo. Which one of you is Ringo? They've got a desk, and they've identified it as Ringo's desk at your old school. . . ."

In the town-hall plaza some 20,000 people were screaming for the Beatles. The Lord Mayor, up for reelection next year, announced he was taking the Beatles to the town-hall ballroom. As he led them up the grand staircase, a police band, concealed below, broke into a Beatle hit, "You Can't Buy Me Love." Ringo danced all the way upstairs. In the second-floor ballroom a noisy crowd of 700 invited guests joined with 400 uninvited guests in storming a long, linen-covered table laden with canapes, cakes and whiskey. When the Beatles entered, accompanied by a single constable, the mob changed direction and attacked them. The Beatles were crushed against the table by the stampede of well-wishers. They were finally rescued by the constable and one of their road managers.

From the town hall the Beatles drove through another cheering mob of 20,000 to the Odean Theater for the local premiere of their film. On the stage of the theater a telegram of congratulations from Prince Philip was read. Offstage, Lord Derby placed a request from Queen Elizabeth for six autographed souvenir programs.

What Brian Epstein has done for them was demonstrated graphically at the London premiere of the Beatles' new movie which took place only a couple of nights before the hoopla in their hometown. There were 12,000 people in Piccadilly Circus. The Beatles' giant faces smiled down nuttily at the originals from the facade of London's Pavillion Theater. Two hundred policemen held the crowd back while the girls chanted "Beatles! Beatles! Beatles!" Several fights broke out. The crowd also sang "Happy Birthday" to Ringo, who was celebrating his 24th the next day. When the Beatles arrived, there was an immense throaty roar. Afterward the theater manager rolled out a newly cleaned red carpet for Princess Margaret. She walked in, tiny and smiling, with her husband, Lord Snowden, trailing behind. The theater was worn and smoky. A detachment of trumpeters blew a tinny fanfare from the stage, and the metropolitan police band played "God Save the Queen." Then the theater darkened, and a short preliminary film colored the screen. It was a travelogue of New Zealand, and the Beatles snickered knowingly. "New Zealand," John said afterward, "is a drag." After that the Beatles were introduced and *A Hard Day's Night* flickered on screen. Later on, when they were presented to the princess, she asked Paul what he thought of the film. "I don't think we are very good, Ma'am," Paul answered, "but we had a very good producer."

What the papers were saying was that Ringo Starr was a movie star as well as a drummer. Not one of the normally dyspeptic London critics could belch up an unkind word about the film. "Another Beatle Success" was the headline in the conservative *Daily Telegraph.* "Ringo," wrote the *Observer*, "emerges as a born actor." And the *Daily Mail* compared the Beatles with the Marx Brothers.   *(1964)*

Haloed with 38 gold records (the record industry's record), the Beatles let the world's hair down, compared themselves with Jesus Christ, played Buckingham Palace where "the Queen treated us like a mum" and altered a generation's way of dressing and thinking. The Liverpudlians made 5 films (appeared on the Post *cover 5 times) and split up while the splitting was good in 1970.*

There'll Never Be Another Elvis

by C. Robert Jennings

A Elvis Presley
B
C Edward G. Robinson
D Eddie Albert
E Richard Chamberlain
F James Garner

So reads the directory of stars in the main dressing-room building on the Metro-Goldwyn-Mayer lot in Culver City, California. Visitors ask the obvious question: "Who is in B?" One touring lady was sure the studio kept B closed in memory of Clark Gable, its most famous occupant. A journalist suggested it was set aside for Greta Garbo, if and when she returned from seclusion. The curious truth is that dressing room B is reserved for the

The "white boy with the black hips" dances in Jailhouse Rock. *Presley initiated royal status and income for pop singers, welded Nashville wax with Negro, folk and "June-moon" tunes, helped create revolutionary climate of '60s.*

Drugs and loneliness contributed to the aging king's un-timely death at 42. Despite becoming a virtual parody of himself, with increasing paunch and wild jump suits, Presley still enjoyed the undiminished enthusiasm of his fans.

small army of young men who surround Elvis Presley. "No other star gets two dressing rooms," sighs a studio executive, "and no one else ever has."

But no one else has ever been a star quite like Elvis Presley. At 30, he is the highest-paid performer in the history of show business. For making four movies and a handful of records this year, he will earn at least $3 million. His 18 films, which cost about $30 million to produce, have already grossed over $175 million.

"Outside of Walt Disney," says Ben Schwalb, producer of Presley's new film, *Tickle Me,* "Elvis is the only sure thing in this business."

When Colonel Tom Parker, Presley's manager, first went to Twentieth Century-Fox—where Elvis made his screen debut—production-boss Buddy Adler delivered a prologue on Elvis's youth and lack of experience. Then he got to the point. "Would $25,000 be all right?" The colonel's eyes studied him incredulously for a moment, then relaxed. "Why, that's just fine for me. Now how about the boy?"

Presley himself is the embodiment of courtesy. "He's the shyest soul I've ever met in this business," exclaims Hedda Hopper. "I say, 'Call me Hedda, Elvis; everybody else does.' He says, 'Yes, ma'am, Mrs. Hopper.' "

Hal Wallis brought Elvis to Hollywood for a screen test and signed him to a seven-year contract which has since been extended. Colonel Parker hired midgets to parade as "The Elvis Presley Midget Fan Club."

Not everyone swooned, and sizable shock waves of outrage swept the country. Leading newspapers denounced him as "lewd and obscene." Ministers mounted whole sermons against him. Other detractors spread stories that his pernicious noise was actually produced, like the noise of the cricket, by some violent stridulation of the legs.

His first film, *Love Me Tender,* opened to unanimous catcalls and jeers from the critics. Yet it earned between five and six times its cost. Critics found his third film, *Jailhouse Rock,* equally obnoxious, and one reviewer commented, sarcastically, that Elvis was "sensitively cast as a slob." Gradually Elvis learned to accept criticism. Today, confronted with a scathing review, he just shrugs and says, "That's the way the mop flops."

Some of Elvis's friends wonder if the constant promotional deals, the records and the heavy schedule of three or four films per year—timed for release during school vacations—aren't beginning to take their toll. "The money is *so* big," one friend exclaims, "that he's always doing what everybody else wants. He's a lonely guy in many ways."

On the surface Elvis remains unruffled. "I always wanted to *be* somebody, and feel like somebody," he explains, "but I never expected to be anybody *important.* I figure if these things bother me too much, though, I could always go back to driving a truck."   *(1965)*

Can You Name This Star?

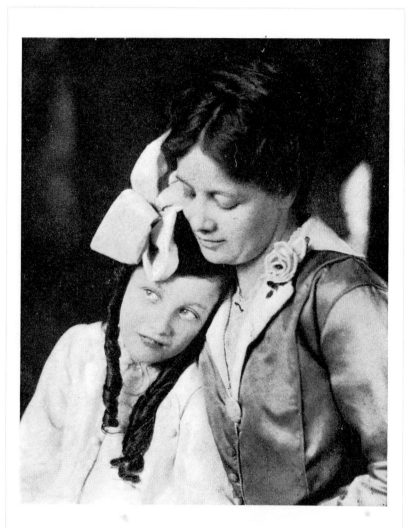

Can You Name This Star?

THIS young lady of ten with the big teeth, hair bow and long curls was born in Texas more than forty years ago. She was christened Lucille, but uses a shorter first name now. She has been married three times—to Douglas Fairbanks, Jr., Franchot Tone and Phillip Terry—and has four adopted children. Her title-role performance in Mildred Pierce won her an Oscar. Can you name her?

—RAYMOND R. STUART.

Answer: Joan Crawford

Can You Name This Star?

THIS poised young lady of seven later became a Hollywood star on the strength of one movie without using a bathing-beauty technique. Born Constance Ockelman in Brooklyn, New York, November 14, 1922, she is the daughter of a German-Danish seaman and a second-generation Irish mother. Although taller than her tiny mother, she weighs only ninety-eight pounds and stands five feet two. A long lock of hair which kept falling over her right eye gave her the allure to win a screen test for I Wanted Wings. The role was seventh down the line in that cast, but it made her famous. Other successes, including I Married a Witch, The Blue Dahlia and Isn't It Romantic, followed. Can you name her?

—RAYMOND R. STUART.

Answer: Veronica Lake.

Can You Name This Star?

THE shirtless youth at left, shown near the old swimming hole on the family ranch in Montana many summers ago, was born in Helena, Montana, but spent his ninth through twelfth years at school in England. As a young man, he sought to become a cartoonist, an artist, and then an advertising salesman. Unsuccessful at all of those, he became a nameless movie extra for more than a year. The first of his many great movies was The Winning of Barbara Worth. Often cast as the rugged Westerner that he actually is, his recent film hits have included Springfield Rifle, High Noon, Blowing Wild and Vera Cruz. Can you name him?   —RAYMOND R. STUART.

Answer: Gary Cooper

Can You Name This Star?

THIS sweet-faced baby with the large, lovely dark eyes, born in New York City on Christmas Day, 1900, would have been a surgeon if he had followed in his father's footsteps. Instead, he became a World War I sailor, a Wall Street messenger, then an actor. Married in 1945 to a well-known movie star, he has a five-year-old son. Equally at home in tough-villain or tough-hero roles, he dates his screen career from The Petrified Forest. His many other hits include To Have and Have Not, Dark Victory, The Maltese Falcon, Casablanca, Key Largo, The Treasure of the Sierra Madre and The Enforcer. Can you name him?
          —RAYMOND R. STUART.

Answer: **Humphrey Bogart.**

Can You Name This Star?

Brooklyn-born Edythe Marrener, of Swedish-Irish-French descent, grew up to model for artists and photographers. She posed for a Saturday Evening Post cover that a movie producer admired. That led to a Hollywood screen test—which, for a time, seemed to lead nowhere. Later, however, she was cast opposite Gary Cooper in Beau Geste. Soon established as a star, the little redhead made screen hits in I'll Cry Tomorrow, The Conqueror, Top-Secret Affair and others. A winsome five feet three and a half and 112 pounds, she married a second time this year after her first marriage ended in divorce. Can you name her?

Raymond R. Stuart

ANSWER:

Susan Hayward

The Noble Tramp
by Joseph Hergesheimer

We stood for a little, talking seriously, in an eddy of bright scented skirts; and, no matter what he said, his face instantly took the form, the emotion, of his words. He had, I thought, the most sensitive face in the world; or rather, its amazing mobility perfectly expressed his most delicate apprehensions. And it was his subconscious, his creative being, never his words, that held me. Intellectually, he was no more interesting than a thousand other vivid inquiring minds, but as himself, as Charlie Chaplin, he had a unique value.

That value had been very widely written about, highly praised, but it hadn't been described with exactitude, perhaps because the medium of its expression was still so

new, so experimental. The moving picture had even been called a new art; but that was nonsense, since if it were an art, it couldn't be new; for all art, at bottom, was no more than a record. The newness of a medium or a very old difficulty—the definition of beauty. For what, at best, Chaplin did was brushed and dignified by beauty. He could make apparent to almost everyone the absurdity of human aspirations; he made tragically and ridiculously clear the unclosable difference between the actuality and the pretense; a grotesque figure in rags, with the ironical emphasis of a cane, impotent, weak, sly, a coward, there yet haunted him dreams and fragments of loveliness and courage. He was always the victim of mishaps that attack not only his pride but the entire self-esteem of civilization; and in the simplest, what well might be called the most vulgar, of ways—he is about to lose his senseless pants in Alaska and he ties them on with a rope—to the other end of which is fastened a dog. And like that, insulted in turn by everyone present, he dances with a girl for whom he has conceived a passionate admiration. An impossible situation; yet, watching it, knowing quite well that, in a moving picture, his pants wouldn't be allowed off, I still felt that they might, in some wretched accident, slip to the floor.

I laughed at Chaplin when I saw him and he was at his best, but when I thought about him I was sober minded. He was, in the shadow of his pantomime transferred to the screen, the most satisfactory actor I had ever seen; he gave me a greater, a more complete, satisfaction than any other; the range of emotions and thoughts he brought up was extraordinary. Mainly, there was that presentation of the brutality of chance I had spoken of, the spectacle of an impotent and conceited atom lost and whirling among the frigid stars. He had this effect on me as well—he clarified to me what I was doing; a small number of works of art had done that and I was immeasurably in their debt. For that, and for more than once, I was indebted to Chaplin. I had said that his mind was not unusual, but it could not have been negligible; it must have had its secret apprehensions, for, at bottom, his great ability was critical; he was a satirist. But his satire—here he was purely creative—lay in actual presentation rather than by a comment on it. He was the veritable waltzing man with a dog tied to his trousers and the girl of his choice mocking him!   *(1926)*

Chaplin found Jackie Coogan in vaudeville, four years old, sharing bows with a song-and-dance papa. The Tramp saw in him the perfect partner; they team here in **The Kid.**

Silent Laughter
by Harold Lloyd

"Once upon a time there was an enchanted city called Los Angeles," is the way this chapter should begin, for in it, under other names, you will find Aladdin, Cinderella, Jack of the Beanstalk, Little Red Riding-Hood, the Sleeping Princess and the poor woodcutter, not to mention the wolf, the giant, the wicked stepmother, the elder sisters, Bluebeard and Big Claus and Little Claus, producers.

A fancy paragraph and open to suspicion of real estate to sell, but an honest heart beats beneath its embroidered waistcoat. It means only that a lot can happen in fifteen years' time in Los Angeles—and has. Bagdad? A mill town with the magic-carpet works shut down.

When I came up from San Diego in the spring of 1913, my father, who was working part time in a shoe store, and I moved into the Belmont, a theatrical hotel on Main Street next to the Hippodrome, a big ten-and-fifteen-cent vaudeville house. Gaylord, who had been homesteading to discouraging results in Wyoming, joined us and became the Belmont's night clerk, while I was bell boy and relief clerk when not making the rounds of the stock companies or bucking the movie extra lines.

The Belmont was populated by small-time vaudeville and stock-burlesque people who bragged or played cards or combined the two hour upon hour in the one public room. Once a Hawaiian band stayed a week. I had been passionately fond of the sob of the steel guitar until then; since, I have gone about slitting the throats of ukuleles and I believe every word of Doctor Rockwell's learned account of the origins of Hawaiian music.

It seems, explains the doctor, that an edict once was issued in Hawaii in the time of the cruel King Kamehameha calling for the death of every male pineapple. Only one escaped. To disguise her man child from the king's ruffians, one loving mamma pineapple pulled the little fellow's whiskers out one by one, and the moaning of the boy pineapple has been preserved in "Aloha Oe" and other native airs.

I was marking time at the Keystone lot in Edendale, where for three weeks they kept me dangling on promises.

"Yes, sir, Lloyd, we are going to give you this and that," they told me daily—and gave me nothing.

As I was on the point of looking elsewhere, they tried me out as an Italian fruitcart vender. I surprised the director with an unexpectedly good makeup, but he was only mildly interested in whether I looked like an Italian peddler or a Norwegian fisherman. The action called for a motorcycle to rip through my fruit cart and for me to take a comedy fall in the midst of the fruit. Could I fall or was I just an upright actor, was the question. Keystone comedies were a series of falls, and Keystoners fell as no one has since Adam and Niagara.

The cart was a breakaway, built in two sections. It burst asunder as the motorcycle charged through, the fruit erupted and I leaped into the air and came down on the back of my neck among oranges and bananas to the critical approval of the director. I was one of them.   *(1928)*

Harold Lloyd specialized in high-flying scenes, dangled from clocks and ledges, seemed helpless in **Safety Last** *but made a fortune buying and selling Hollywood property.*

Banjo Eyes
by Eddie Cantor

Though the thought of living in Hollywood thrilled my children, they were reluctant to leave our home in Mount Vernon, where they had built up pleasant friendships and associations. I tried to comfort them.

"Look who your new friends will be! I'll have Gloria Swanson play jacks with you and you'll skip rope with Vilma Banky!"

Margie, my oldest, was skeptical. "Yeh! And I suppose you'll get Norma Shearer to wait on us at table!"

But when I suggested that we leave three weeks before school closed they were promptly converted.

On arriving in Los Angeles, we rented a bungalow in Beverly Hills and left the door open for Chaplin, Fairbanks

and Rin-Tin-Tin to walk in. But Margie says the only regular caller we had was the landlord.

Personally I looked forward to my Hollywood visit with a good deal of excitement. I had read so much about this hell's kitchen in the newspapers that I brought along a one-piece bathing suit to wear to banquets. I expected to see a repetition of the old Roman days when emperors threw parties on the street and half-naked men and women caroused on beds of roses. Instead, it turned out to be a small factory town, very provincial and terribly industrious. For the first time in my life I had to wake up at dawn and get into makeup so I could be shot at sunrise.

The director knew that I was accustomed to play before audiences and that their laughter would stimulate my sense of ad-libbing. To help me along in those scenes, he collected a crowd of onlookers and they laughed at so much per day. I never got so many laughs in my life.

But there were also serious moments in the production. One of them was when I had to kiss Clara Bow. It seems we got everything right but that, and we had to do it over and over again. And when Clara kisses you, you have been osculated!

In the cliff scene of *Kid Boots*, which made the movie audiences gasp, doubles were used for both Clara Bow and myself. Only once did I double for myself, and heartily regretted it.

The picture showed me being dragged along the ground by a galloping horse with a rope around my waist. When this shot was taken I was tied, not to the galloping horse but to a slow-moving automobile, the director alongside me in a moving camera truck. While I was running, supposedly pulled by the frantic steed, the director told me to skip gracefully.

I tried it and fell. The automobile dragged me some distance over the rough road before it was stopped. My knees were bleeding and gravel had cut my hands, lodging deep under the skin. I had to spend several hours getting the gravel removed. If I needed sand to make good in pictures, I surely got enough then for the rest of my career.

When the picture was finally completed, and while it was still being studied in the projection room for cuts and revisions, I lost no time in getting my tickets for New York, figuring that they could never really hurt a man three thousand miles away.   *(1932)*

Cantor in Ziegfeld's Kid Boots. *Eddie created style of light, comic banter, inspired Will Rogers to do same.*

Artful Codger

by Alva Johnston

The beautiful perfidiousness and fraudulency of the Fields of the screen originated out of necessity. Sinister work at the card table in his formative years gave his face a mask of aggravated innocence. Explaining things to magistrates caused him to cultivate that look of a startled altar boy which still survives in a Falstaffian way. The admiration that Fields received during his adolescence for petty crimes and misdemeanors has greatly influenced his ideas of comedy. He was envied by acquaintances who feared to do what he did. Today he thinks that the public has all the makings of a thief or confidence man, but is more or less crushed under the iron heel of respectability. Most of the Fields comedy is built to appeal to the dormant larceny and chicanery of audiences. The average man, it seems, experiences a feeling of glory and exaltation as he identifies himself with the comedian when Fields cheats a landlady, robs a sucker with a marked deck, shortchanges a yokel, sells a gold brick or steals a silk hat.

Hollywood in general is supposed to regard the public as a case of arrested development. Bill thinks the public intelligent, but a moral delinquent. Hence a deep spiritual kinship naturally arises between the spectators and the grand old reprobate on the screen. Fields panders to their nostalgia for disreputableness. In a way, Bill is a muckraker or reformer; he gets his laughs by exposing the petty crime in the audience's bosom. The more you laugh at Fields the more police attention you need.

The Hays organization is more tolerant of rum than it used to be, but even when it was a stronghold of teetotalism it never attempted to take the bottle away from Fields. There was a rule against alcohol; there was a still stronger rule against attacking national institutions. In the case of Fields, the rules canceled each other. The Hays organization was forced to take the position that whisky guzzled by Bill Fields was null and void. His heroic drinking scenes, like many of his other reprehensible activities on the screen, are highly autobiographical. A physician testified on the witness stand in Los Angeles last year that Fields formerly drank two quarts of whisky a day. This would have been considered disastrous publicity for any other star. Fields regarded it as a buildup. In his radio appearance on the following Sunday, his stooge inquired, "Mr. Fields, what would your father have said if he knew that you drank two bottles of whisky a day?" "He would

have said that I was a sissy," replied Fields.

During his boyhood Fields had to solve the problem of self-preservation nearly every day. This cultivated in him one of the most distinguished senses of self-preservation to be found in the world. His writers say that Fields tries to seize every good thing in a picture, and his ideal of a motion-picture masterpiece is a ten-reel Fields soliloquy. It all goes back to the days when Fields was the most agile milk thief in Philadelphia and its environs. At that time he was peppered several times by rock salt. He was much bitten by dogs and other fauna. The old rock-salt and watchdog scars still ache, and the struggle for survival is fiercer in Fields today than ever. *(1932)*

Fields and Margaret Hamilton (of Wicked Witch and Maxwell House). Miss Hamilton traded teaching for acting.

Monkey Business
by Arthur Marx

When we returned to Hollywood in the fall, Chico reported that Irving Thalberg of MGM was anxious to have lunch with the Marx brothers. They met at the Beverly Wilshire Hotel on the following day. Father asked the producer what he thought of their pictures, *Monkey Business* and *Horsefeathers*.

"They were very funny pictures," answered Thalberg. "The trouble was they had no stories. It's better to be not so funny and have a story that the audience is interested in. For my money, comedy scenes have to further the plot. They have to be helping someone who's a sympathetic character. Then your pictures would be twice as good, and you'd gross three times as much."

"Well, I didn't come here to be insulted," said father. "I'd rather have lunch by myself somewhere else. If you want to talk a deal, that's something else again."

Ultimatums, yet!

Harpo and Chico exchanged nervous glances and wished their brother would keep his big trap shut for a change.

But Thalberg was more interested in signing them than he had let on. "No offense," he said to father, with a smile, "I just thought it would be better for the four of us to understand each other before we actually started working together. If you're willing to go along with my theories, I think it can be very profitable for all of us."

Soon after the Marx brothers moved into their office on the Metro lot, a secretary phoned, telling them to be in Thalberg's bungalow-office for a story conference at three o'clock. Promptly at the appointed time the three of them trooped into Thalberg's reception room only to be told by the secretary that the producer wouldn't be able to see them until he had finished reading a script.

When a half hour had gone by and Thalberg still hadn't asked for them, father and his brothers were fuming.

"How do you like that guy?" said father. "Who does he think he is—Irving Thalberg?"

"I could have had a bridge game this afternoon," said Chico wistfully.

"We've got to do something," said Harpo.

After a hurried conference, father and his brothers lit cigars and blew clouds of smoke under Thalberg's door. Pretty soon Thalberg noticed the smoke, and imagining that his reception room was on fire, he rushed to the door to investigate. As he peered out, father and his brothers stuck their feet in the doorway.

Another time they had an appointment with Thalberg for three o'clock, and were still waiting at five-thirty, when the secretary left for home. Her parting instructions were, "Just be patient; he'll see you any hour now."

But their patience was exhausted. As soon as the secretary was out of sight, they shoved her desk in front of Thalberg's door, collected all the heavy steel filing cabinets in the room and piled them on top of the desk. Then they went home. It took Thalberg an hour to escape, and after that he took care to keep appointments with the Marx brothers on time.   *(1954)*

Margaret DuMont, practically a member of the Marx family, submits to her usual martyrdom with Groucho in **Duck Soup**, *a film that repeated an earlier stage success.*

Say "Cheese"
by Eddie Cantor

I know one star in Hollywood who hasn't been spoiled by success, and that is Mickey Mouse. I knew Mickey when he was just a little rat around the studios. He'd sneak out of his hole in the wall, bum a piece of cheese from one of the extras, and run back into the plaster. Nobody wanted to give him a chance in pictures. Today Mickey Mouse owns the showplace of Beverly Hills, has three Japanese butlers, four imported cars and his own cheese mill right in back of the house.

I attended a party at his home the other night and all the stars of Hollywood were there. They wouldn't think of refusing an invitation from Mickey Mouse. Even Professor Albert Einstein, who has made several visits to the movie colony, was honored to attend. I noticed him on the patio, talking to a blue-eyed platinum blonde.

The platinum baby tried to impress Einstein with her knowledge and said dreamily, "Isn't Mars beautiful!"

"That isn't Mars; that's Venus," said Einstein.

"Oh, professor, it's marvelous how you can tell their sex from this distance!"

I quickly slipped inside to talk with Mickey. In spite of all the wealth and splendor which success has brought him, he's the same old little mouse. He's very democratic, and once in a while he drops into holes in the wall to play with less fortunate mice. Only, of course, now the holes are made of pink tile with built-in showers. Mickey told me the most thrilling experience he ever had. One night, some years ago, he came home late from the studio and a cat who didn't know he was Mickey Mouse nearly ate him. He told the cat who he was. She apologized and opened her mouth to let him out. The next day he gave her a job on his lot, and now she is none other than Krazy Kat. He thinks there is a big future in the talkies for cats and mice. I like Mickey because he's a chap who doesn't deny his race.

He writes his own stuff, directs his own pictures, and he and Minnie Mouse supply all the actors they can use right from their own family. For all the breathtaking stunts he does, Mickey never employs a double. Minnie just sews his tail for him after each performance and he's all set again. He gets a thousand proposals of marriage a day by mail, but there's no girl like Minnie! Mickey is the most home-loving star in Hollywood. He never goes out except to give a success talk at the Mouse Night School or be the judge at a Mouse Beauty Contest.

The only time Mickey got excited was when I asked him about movie censorship. He told me that in his last picture the censors made him put a skirt on one horse, his dog had to wear pajamas and all the birds were dressed in step-ins. He had a passionate love scene between two coconut trees, but he had to take it over and make the trees put on raccoon coats. In another scene Minnie had to bathe the baby with its clothes on and the centipede walked around with a hundred and twenty-four pairs of pants.   *(1932)*

Disney got the idea from a "particularly friendly" mouse who lived in his wastebasket when Walt worked at his drawing board late at night. "Mortimer Mouse! It has a swing," Disney said to his wife. But she wasn't buying. "All right, how about Mickey?" he asked.

Post 'toons

"Just wait until the kissing scenes."

"All right! Break it up—break it up!"

"I knew I'd seen it before—it's a re-release of The Birth of a Nation!*"*

"The balcony is filled too, but I have a box I can put you in."

I've Created
a Monster

by Richard G. Hubler

The all-time master artist of the horrifics was an energetic perfectionist named Lon Chaney. He first became famous as the cripple in the movie production of *The Miracle Man*. By adapting his vaudeville talents as a contortionist, Chaney won supremacy as a horrifier. In his versions of *The Hunchback of Notre Dame* and *The Phantom of the Opera*, Chaney set national heart-failure records.

Other horror classics enjoyed a revival after Chaney. John Barrymore appeared in *Dr. Jekyll and Mr. Hyde*. So did Fredric March. This perennial was redone recently by Metro-Goldwyn-Mayer, starring Spencer Tracy. Charles Laughton took a shot at *The Hunchback of Notre Dame* a few years ago.

The critics unanimously and invariably pan all horror pictures. When the grosses come in, the producers say defiantly, "We make pictures that nobody but the audience likes."

Yet horrifics merit some artistic credit. They employ excellent actors. Basil Rathbone has dabbled in them. So has Claude Rains. In the first *Frankenstein*, John Boles and Mae Clarke—who achieved more fame when James Cagney pushed a half grapefruit in her face—were the straights. Colin Clive, a fine actor, was Doctor Frankenstein. There seems to be a need for an English accent somewhere in each horrific. Clipped tones put a cultured patina on the melodrama and somehow make it more believable. Incidentally, England always has been the best foreign market for horror pictures.

The chief problem in the horrifics is the resurrection of the heroes. The formula decrees that they must die the most horrible death imaginable and then have a logical reincarnation. Frankenstein, for example, has (1) fallen into a burning inferno, (2) been blown to bits, (3) buried in a pit of molten lava, and (4) crushed under falling timbers. But he's up and about again, hale as ever.

George Waggner, the one entrusted with production of most of Universal's chillers, thinks next time he'll drown the monster in boiling water. Lon Chaney, Jr., who has lived up to his famous father's reputation, came to him with a suggestion after the last production.

Hungarian Bela Lugosi portrayed the ultimate villain, Count Dracula of Transylvania, in memorable 1931 film.

"Say," he said enthusiastically, "let's have *The Ghost of Frankenstein* end with the monster melting down before your eyes in the fire!"

"Fine," growled Waggner. "Great! And what do we start the next *Frankenstein* with? A grease spot?"

"All I want to see," one horror writer confided, "is the horror picture to end all horror pictures. It should be called *Frankenstein Meets Mickey Rooney*. And I don't care how it comes out!"   *(1942)*

Scream Gems

by John Kobler

The gimmick William Castle contrived for "*McKabra*," as he pronounces it, involved the services of Lloyd's of London. Before he had even hit upon a sufficiently gruesome story to film, he applied to the venerable insurance firm for a blanket policy covering any member of the audience who died of fright, the beneficiary to receive $1,000. After some debate over the propriety of such a transaction, Lloyd's actuaries solemnly computed the statistically probable number of casualties to be five, and the policy was issued at a premium of $5,000.

Upon this fragile foundation Castle erected a tower of trumpery. At the box office the preponderantly adolescent customers were handed "beneficiary agreements" to

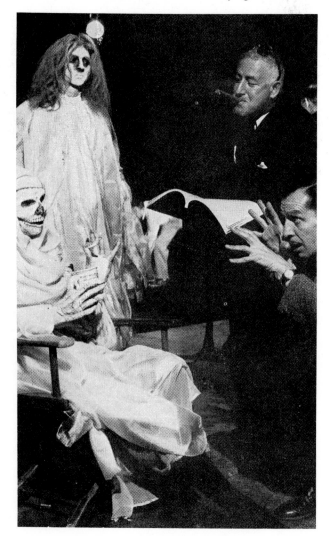

fill out. In the lobby, by a medicine chest, a model wearing a nurse's uniform dispensed "nerve-steadying pills."

The Tingler, with its accompanying gimmick, "Percepto," Castle considers his masterwork. "Today," he announced in an invitation to the Hollywood press during the shooting last spring, "the stages at Columbia Studios, where the Tingler has been loose for two days, will be open. The Tingler is still on stage, but safely locked up. However, this unpredictable mass of pent-up fury that soars beyond the wildest flights of your nightmare fantasies, may somehow escape from bondage. For this reason, every visitor to *The Tingler* set will be insured for $100,000."

A variant of the hoary "mad scientist" theme, the movie revolves around the notion that fear breeds a living organism in the victim's spine—the Tingler—which, if not nullified, will shatter the vertebrae. The only way to nullify it is to scream. The scientist who harbors this dotty theory, hammed up by Vincent Price as few but Price can ham it, resolves to isolate the Tingler so he can study it in the laboratory. But what sort of victim would be incapable of screaming? A mute, of course. Such a subject the doctor finds in Judith Evelyn, whose husband operates a movie theater. Scared to death by a series of induced hallucinations, including bathtub taps that run blood, Miss Evelyn ends up on Price's dissecting table. Presently a crawfishlike creature slithers to the floor, escapes and proceeds to stalk other victims. A reel later it breaks into the bereaved husband's theater during a performance and assaults the projectionist.

At that point, in the actual theater, the screen goes blank; and through directional loudspeakers pours Price's malted-milk voice, "Ladies and gentlemen, please do not panic, but scream, scream for your lives! The Tingler is loose in this theater, and if you don't scream, it may kill you!" The juveniles usually comply, while the loudspeakers project general hysteria—"It's on me! Help! . . . Look out, it's under your seat!" What touches off the climactic pandemonium is Percepto, a hookup of low-voltage electric motors beneath the seats that buzz the occupants.

In the Chicago neighborhood theaters *The Tingler* outsold *Anatomy of a Murder* and *Gigi*, both widely acclaimed films. "Now that's wrong—what's the matter with people?" Castle wonders happily.　　*(1960)*

Price and his fiendish friends jolted audiences out of their seats with help from a gimmick called Percepto.

Memoirs of Frankenstein

by Boris Karloff

It is not true that I was born a monster. Hollywood made me one. That was thirty-one years ago, and I have lived menacingly ever after. While some potential victims have eluded my fangs, claws and other assorted horrors, I have found it almost impossible to escape monster roles.

I wandered into movies, via a five-dollar-a-day extra role as a swarthy Mexican soldier in a Doug Fairbanks, Sr., film, *His Majesty, The American.* For the next eight or nine years, I played extra and small featured roles when things were good, loaded cement sacks in warehouses when they weren't. At 42 I was an obscure actor playing obscure parts. I quit writing home—for I had nothing to write about.

My big break came while I was downing a sandwich-and-tea lunch in the Universal commissary. After a string of sweet-and-kindly roles, I had played the diabolical Galloway, the convict-killer in *The Criminal Code.* Someone tapped me on the shoulder and said, "Mr. Whale would like to see you at his table." Jimmy Whale was the most important director on the lot. "We're getting ready to shoot the Mary Shelley classic, *Frankenstein*," Whale said, "and I'd like you to test—for the monster."

It was a bit shattering, but I felt that any part was better than no part at all. The studio's head makeup man, Jack Pierce, spent evenings experimenting with me. Slowly, under his skillful touch, the monster's double-domed forehead, sloping brow, flattened Neanderthal eyelids and surgical scars materialized. A week later I was ready for the test. I readily passed as a monster.

The scene where the monster was created, amid booming thunder and flashing lightning, made me as uneasy as anyone. For while I lay half-naked and strapped to Doctor Frankenstein's table, I could see directly above me the special-effects men brandishing the white-hot scissorslike carbons that made the lightning. I hoped that no one up there had butterfingers.

Frankenstein finally was released for its premiere on December 6, 1931, at Santa Barbara. I was not even invited and had never seen it. I was just an unimportant free-lance actor, the animation for the monster costume.

Boris played the immortal monster only three times and became irrevocably identified as Frankenstein thereafter.

Frankenstein transformed not only my life but also the film industry. It grossed something like $12 million on a $250,000 investment, started a cycle of so-called boy-meets-ghoul horror films and quickly made its producers realize they'd made a dreadful mistake. They let the monster die in the burning mill. In one brief script conference, however, they brought him back alive. It seems he had only fallen through the flaming floor into the pond and could now go on for reels and reels.   *(1962)*

Sympathy for the Devil

by Gwen Dobson

When Father John J. Nicola was appointed consultant on the film *The Exorcist*, he viewed it as simply another facet of his study which commenced during his seminary days.

The fact that Father Nicola was then assistant director of the National Shrine of the Immaculate Conception, added practicality to the matter.

In harmony with his knowledge of the subject was his familiarity with the actual case upon which the book was based . . . the documented and witnessed and verified case of a fourteen-year-old Mount Rainier, Maryland, boy.

The 1949 case had been well followed and reported in the Washington press after a journalistic wrestling match between the Irish Catholic reporter who wanted to write the account and the Irish Catholic managing editor, who didn't want him to but finally yielded. The editor did not question the story on the basis of its veracity but rather on its impact.

And that today is the prime concern of the priest-consultant.

He knew during the shooting that the film would draw criticism. He knew that many older Catholics, steeped in their childhood knowledge of the Catechism, would react bitterly against certain scenes and he tried, often in vain, to soften them. He fought to protect sensitivities and he fought to shade several of the scenes which he felt would be repugnant. All the while, though, he had to stand his ground against a director, William Friedkin, for whom he had great respect.

The director felt he had a duty to be faithful to the book and the priest felt as strongly he had a duty to the potential audience, whose reaction admittedly would be mixed.

So ambivalent was Father Nicola that he rejected two acting offers in the film as a quiet protest and a silent statement that he did not give his full approval.

The phone rings. Catholics are incensed that he had any part of the film . . . others call, claiming the need of an exorcist. And Father Nicola worries that the film could produce a wave of hysteria which he likens to the periods of witchcraft and witch-hunts. "Such mass hysteria is possible and it could produce an outbreak of what is thought to be demonic influence. The book itself resulted in some eight or nine cases of pseudo-possession. I know of about 100 such cases and in most instances they were teenagers who had read the book, identified with it and began acting it out."   *(1974)*

Priests waged war against the devil and the director in **The Exorcist** *as the advisor/priest to the film fought to lessen its horrifying impact. Catholics protested, audiences fainted; both waited in block-long lines to see the show.*

Sales Dept.

RKO
PRESENTS

DOUGLAS FAIRBANKS, Jr.
MAUREEN O'HARA · WALTER SLEZAK
in
SINBAD the SAILOR
with ANTHONY QUINN · GEORGE TOBIAS
JANE GREER · MIKE MAZURKI
Produced by STEPHEN AMES · Directed by RICHARD WALLACE
Screen Play by JOHN TWIST
in Glorious Technicolor

Jeanette MacDonald had an enchanting voice and fairy-tale looks, brought light opera and brilliant music to the screen. Here she dances with Maurice Chevalier, a French import who never wore out his welcome in 40 years.

Like other Broadway show stoppers, Irving Berlin had plenty to give and to sell Hollywood.

Among the various genres of American art, the poster—called "that most earthbound of the visual communicators" by curator Margaret Cogswell of the National Collection of Fine Arts—pleads a most direct and immediate message, at once passionate, complex, contradictory, vigorous. "Posters are authentic images of an era," she writes. "They are signposts which tell us much about where we have been; who did them, how and why, furnish clues as to where we are going."

The success of the poster as advertising was stunningly apparent as early as the earliest movies, and many of the masterpieces were produced by the most talented artists of the time. Ads derived much of their visual vocabulary from regional folk art, held attention with the purely visual idea—most often photographic, sometimes incorporating comic-strip stylistics, or other popular imagery. Modern celebrities in TV ads are direct descendants of Rita Hayworth announcing with a smile that "all my friends know Chesterfield is my brand," or Joan Crawford, who drinks Coca-Cola and says "you must feel a smile to act one." Or Clara Bow, Eddie Cantor, Adolphe Menjou at Paramount, who will "enchant you and thrill you with laughter, romance and excitement!" ("If it's a Paramount Picture, it's the best show in town.")

Some of the country's most extravagant ad campaigns were developed for film promotion. *Dinner at Eight*, with Jean Harlow and Wallace Beery, had one of the largest promotions in history. New York City department stores

Paramount advertises. Harold Lloyd lost two fingers, hanging from ledges and camera men thereafter had to show him clinging with his opposite hand. Clara Bow, the "It" girl, was created by studio publicity people, starting a trend in which image gained ascendancy over talent though Miss Bow had plenty of "it." Eddie Cantor said Will Rogers was the "comic policeman of America" and that none of the shenanigans of present-day Washington could take place if Rogers were alive.

decorated their windows as sets with life-size cutout figures of stars. Table settings said *Dinner at Eight*. Dresses were designed after costumes from the movie. In fact, one store went so far as to have an entire section of movie-costume wardrobes available to star-struck shoppers.

Who doesn't recall as a child gazing up at splendid marquee smiles of Judy Garland dancing with Fred Astaire in Irving Berlin's *Easter Parade*, the intense gaze of Maureen O'Hara as she points a knife at a laughing, dashing Douglas Fairbanks, Jr., in *Sinbad the Sailor?*

John Garrigan, American art authority, said posters have always been "an indicator of culture. . . . a great poster often becomes the symbol of a product, cause, or event. A synthesis of message and method, it can shock or entertain, stir the emotions, and linger in the memory." The greats of the movie posters, as a means of communication, are still unsurpassed.

Today, movie poster art is high camp and sold by department store interior decorating departments, campus bookstores, art and print shops. Some deal exclusively in movie posters and ads with prices ranging upwards to hundreds of dollars. Full-sized billboards are available as murals to cover entire walls. The magic of the show, obviously, goes on.

A NEW HIGH IN THE MOVIE SKY. M-G-M PRESENTS IN VistaVISION AND COLOR
A SOL C. SIEGEL PRODUCTION
starring
BING CROSBY · GRACE KELLY · FRANK SINATRA
in the hilarious low-down on high life
"HIGH SOCIETY"
co-starring
CELESTE HOLM · JOHN LUND · LOUIS CALHERN · SIDNEY BLACKMER
and **LOUIS ARMSTRONG** AND HIS BAND
Screen Play by JOHN PATRICK · Based on a Play by Philip Barry · Music and Lyrics by **COLE PORTER**
Music Supervised and Adapted by JOHNNY GREEN and SAUL CHAPLIN · Color by TECHNICOLOR · Directed by CHARLES WALTERS · An M-G-M Picture

Are YOU a MITTY?

CAN you, like Danny Kaye, daydream yourself as a daring ace? Can you become seven different personalities in your daydreams? Does the girl of your daydreams ever come true, like Virginia Mayo? How would you like to be frightened by Boris Karloff, hen-pecked by Fay Bainter, pursued by Ann Rutherford, and adored by the gorgeous Goldwyn Girls? You, too, can be a Mitty if you try! Samuel Goldwyn, who gave you "The Best Years Of Our Lives," now gives you *the best time of your life* in "The Secret Life Of Walter Mitty," photographed in Technicolor by Lee Garmes, directed by Norman McLeod and sparkling with matchless music.

Entertainment in the Goldwyn manner

(Opposite) **Post** *writer Joel Chandler Harris' Aesopic Uncle Remus characters came to the screen with Walt Disney's gentle touch. (Above) Louis Armstrong stole the show with his brass rubbings while Sinatra and Crosby harmonized as sweetly as choir boys to Cole Porter's songs in a musical version of* **The Philadelphia Story.**

"I love the idea of there being two sexes, don't you?" James Thurber asked. His archetypal dreamer, Walter Mitty, loved the idea of there being heroes and history and Virginia Mayo. Danny Kaye, dancer, singer, jokester, played the role of Thurber's abstraction with great wit and personality.

JOHN FORD'S MASTERPIECE

JOHN FORD and MERIAN C. COOPER

present

JOHN WAYNE
HENRY FONDA
SHIRLEY TEMPLE
PEDRO ARMENDARIZ

FORT APACHE

Directed by
JOHN FORD

Screen play by Frank Nugent
as suggested by The Saturday Evening Post
story "Massacre" by James Warner Bellah
AN ARGOSY PICTURE
Released thru RKO Radio Pictures, Inc.

A real picture and a great one.
cavalrymen . . . their women . .

JOHN WAYNE	HENRY FONDA	SHIRLEY TEMPLE	PEDRO ARMENDARIZ	WARD BOND	GEORGE O'BRIEN	VICTOR McLAGLEN
as Capt. York	as Colonel Thursday	as Philadelphia Thursday	as Sergeant Beaufort	as Sergeant O'Rourke	as Capt. Collingwood	as Sergeant Mulcahy

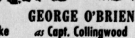

OF THE FRONTIER!

It's got sweep and scope, human scenes straight from the shoulder. There are long, le...
...fighting...humor. You can smell the heat and the dust. In other words, this is motion pictu...

ANNA LEE
as Mrs. Collingwood

IRENE RICH
as Mrs. O'Rourke

DICK FORAN
as Sergeant Quincannon

GUY KIBBEE
as Dr. Wilkins

GRANT WITHERS
as Meacham

MAE MARSH
as Mrs. Gates

and introducing
JOHN AGAR
as Mickey O'Rourke

Capra's movies were positive and convincingly possible. Audiences believed Mr. Smith could go to Washington and do something, or that Jimmy Stewart and Donna Reed could create permanent happiness through a kiss. Film also starred giants Lionel Barrymore and Beulah Bondi. Capra specialized in using character actors in his films.

Screen queen Joan Crawford said she never went out in public without dressing the part of a great star.

Rita Hayworth, spectacular as a Colorado sunrise, married Aly Khan, became one of many film stars to wed royalty.

Post
Movie Stories

Babylon Revisited
by F. Scott Fitzgerald

"And where's Mr. Campbell?" Charlie asked.

"Gone to Switzerland. Mr. Campbell's a pretty sick man, Mr. Wales."

"I'm sorry to hear that. And George Hardt?" Charlie inquired.

"Back in America, gone to work."

"And where is the snow bird?"

"He was in here last week. Anyway, his friend, Mr. Schaeffer, is in Paris."

Two familiar names from the long list of a year and a half ago. Charlie scribbled an address in his notebook and tore out the page.

"If you see Mr. Schaeffer, give him this," he said. "It's my brother-in-law's address. I haven't settled on a hotel yet."

He was not really disappointed to find Paris so empty. But the stillness in the bar was strange, almost portentous. It was not an American bar anymore—he felt polite in it, and not as if he owned it. It had gone back to France. He had felt the stillness from the moment he got out of the taxi and saw the doorman, usually in a frenzy of activity at this hour, gossiping with a *chasseur* by the servant's entrance.

Passing through the corridor, he heard only a single, bored voice in the once-clamorous women's room. When he turned into the bar he traveled the twenty feet of green carpet with his eyes fixed straight ahead by old habit; and then, with his foot firmly on the rail, he turned and surveyed the room, encountering only a single pair of eyes that fluttered up from a newspaper in the corner. Charlie asked for the head barman, Paul, who in the latter days of the bull market had come to work in his own custom-built car—disembarking, however, with due nicety at the nearest corner. But Paul was at his country house today and Alix was giving him his information.

"No, no more. I'm going slow these days."

Alix congratulated him: "Hope you stick to it, Mr. Wales. You were going pretty strong a couple of years ago."

"I'll stick to it all right," Charlie assured him. "I've stuck to it for over a year and a half now."

"How do you find conditions in America?"

"I haven't been to America for months. I'm in business in Prague, representing a couple of concerns there. They don't know about me down there." He smiled faintly. "Remember the night of George Hardt's bachelor dinner here? . . . By the way, what's become of Claude Fessenden?"

Alix lowered his voice confidentially: "He's in Paris, but he doesn't come here anymore. Paul doesn't allow it. He ran up a bill of thirty thousand francs, charging all his drinks and his lunches, and usually his dinner, for more than a year. And when Paul finally told him he had to pay, he gave him a bad check."

Alix pressed his lips together and shook his head.

"I don't understand it, such a dandy fellow. Now he's all bloated up——" He made a plump apple of his hands.

A thin world, resting on a common weakness, shredded away now like tissue paper. Turning, Charlie saw a group of effeminate young men installing themselves in a corner.

"Nothing affects them," he thought. "Stocks rise and fall, people loaf or work, but they go on forever." The place oppressed him. He called for the dice and shook with Alix for the drink.

"Here for long, Mr. Wales?"

"I'm here for four or five days to see my little girl."

"Oh-h! You have a little girl?"

Outside, the fire-red, gas-blue, ghost-green signs shone smokily through the tranquil rain. It was late afternoon and the streets were in movement; the *bistros* gleamed. At the corner of the Boulevard des Capucines he took a taxi. The Place de la Concorde moved by in pink majesty; they crossed the logical Seine, and Charlie felt the sudden provincial quality of the left bank.

"I spoiled this city for myself," he thought. "I didn't realize it, but the days came along one after another, and then two years were gone, and everything was gone, and I was gone."

He was thirty-five, a handsome man, with the Irish mobility of his face sobered by a deep wrinkle between his eyes. As he rang his brother-in-law's bell in the Rue Palatine, the wrinkle deepened till it pulled down his brows; he felt a cramping sensation in his belly. From behind the maid who opened the door darted a lovely little girl of nine who shrieked "Daddy!" and flew up, struggling like a fish, into his arms. She pulled his head around by one ear and set her cheek against his.

"My old pie," he said.

"Oh, daddy, daddy, daddy, daddy, dads, dads, dads!"

She drew him into the salon, where the family waited, a boy and girl his daughter's age, his sister-in-law and her husband. He greeted Marion with his voice pitched care-

"Babylon Revisited" became The Last Time I Saw Paris *(Van Johnson, Elizabeth Taylor), and something was lost in translation.*

fully to avoid either feigned enthusiasm or dislike, but her response was more frankly tepid, and she minimized her expression of unshakable distrust by directing her regard toward his child. The two men clasped hands in a friendly way and Lincoln Peters rested his for a moment on Charlie's shoulder.

The room was warm and comfortably American. The three children moved intimately about, playing through the yellow oblongs that led to other rooms; the cheer of six o'clock spoke in the eager smacks of the fire and the sounds of French activity in the kitchen. But Charlie did not relax; his heart sat up rigidly in his body and he drew confidence from his daughter, who from time to time came close to him, holding in her arms the doll he had brought.

"Really extremely well," he declared in answer to Lincoln's question. "There's a lot of business there that isn't moving at all, but we're doing even better than ever. In fact, damn well. I'm bringing my sister over from America next month to keep house for me. In fact, my income is bigger than it was when I had money. You see, the Czechs——"

His boasting was for a specific purpose; but after a moment, seeing a faint restiveness in Lincoln's eye, he changed the subject:

"Those are fine children of yours, well brought up, good manners."

"We think Honoria's a great little girl too."

Marion Peters came back into the little salon. She was a tall woman with worried eyes, who had once possessed a fresh American loveliness. Charlie had never been sensitive to it and was always surprised when people spoke of how pretty she had been. From the first there had been an instinctive antipathy between them.

"Well, how do you find Honoria?" she asked.

"Wonderful. I was astonished how much she's grown in ten months. All the children are looking well."

"We haven't had a doctor for a year. How do you like being back in Paris?"

"It seems very funny to see so few Americans around."

"I'm delighted," Marion said vehemently. "Now at least you can go into a store without their assuming you're a millionaire. We've suffered like everybody, but on the whole it's a good deal pleasanter."

"But it was nice while it lasted," Charlie said. "We were a sort of royalty, almost infallible, with a sort of magic around us. In the bar this afternoon"—he stumbled, seeing his mistake—"there wasn't a man I knew."

She looked at him keenly. "I should think you'd have had enough of bars."

"I only stayed a minute. I take one drink every afternoon, and no more."

"Don't you want a cocktail before dinner?" Lincoln asked.

"I take only one drink every afternoon, and I've had that."

"I hope you keep to it," said Marion.

Her dislike was evident in the coldness with which she spoke, but Charlie only smiled; he had larger plans. Her very aggressiveness gave him an advantage, and he knew enough to wait. He wanted them to initiate the discussion of what they knew had brought him to Paris.

Honoria was to spend the following afternoon with him. At dinner he couldn't decide whether she was most like him or her mother. Fortunate if she didn't combine the traits of both that had brought them to disaster. A great wave of protectiveness went over him. He thought he knew what to do for her. He believed in character; he wanted to jump back a whole generation and trust in character again as the eternally valuable element. Everything wore out now. Parents expected genius, or at least brilliance, and both the forcing of children and the fear of forcing them, the fear of warping natural abilities, were poor substitutes for that long, careful watchfulness, that checking and balancing and reckoning of accounts, the end of which was that there should be no slipping below a certain level of duty and integrity.

That was what the elders had been unable to teach plausibly since the break between the generations ten or twelve years ago.

He left soon after dinner, but not to go home. He was curious to see Paris by night with clearer and more judicious eyes. He bought a *strapontin* for the Casino and watched Josephine Baker go through her chocolate arabesques.

After an hour he left and strolled toward Montmartre, up the Rue Pigalle into the Place Blanche. The rain had stopped and there were a few people in evening clothes disembarking from taxis in front of cabarets, and *cocottes* prowling singly or in pairs, and many Negroes. He passed a lighted door from which issued music, and stopped with the sense of familiarity; it was Bricktop's, where he had parted with so many hours and so much money. A few doors farther on he found another ancient rendezvous and incautiously put his head inside. Immediately an eager orchestra burst into sound, a pair of professional dancers leaped to their feet and a maître d' hôtel swooped toward him, crying, "Crowd just arriving, sir!" But he withdrew quickly.

"You have to be damn drunk," he thought.

Zeilli's was closed, the bleak and sinister cheap hotels surrounding it were dark; up in the Rue Blanche there was more light and a local, colloquial French crowd. The Poet's Cave had disappeared, but the two great mouths of the Café of Heaven and the Café of Hell still yawned—even devoured, as he watched, the meager contents of a tourist bus—a German, a Japanese, and an American couple who glanced at him with frightened eyes.

So much for the effort and ingenuity of Montmartre. All the catering to vice and waste was on an utterly childish scale, and he suddenly realized the meaning of the word "dissipate"—to dissipate into thin air; to make nothing out of something. In the little hours of the night every move from place to place was an enormous human

Elizabeth Taylor (with Roger Moore) had everything:
great beauty, talent and six husbands.

jump, an increase of paying for the privilege of slower and
slower motion.

He remembered thousand-franc notes given to an orchestra for playing a single number, hundred-franc notes
tossed to a doorman for calling a cab.

But it hadn't been given for nothing.

It had been given, even the most wildly squandered
sum, as an offering to destiny that he might not remember
the things most worth remembering, the things that now
he would always remember—his child taken from his control, his wife escaped to a grave in Vermont.

In the glare of a *brasserie* a woman spoke to him. He
bought her some eggs and coffee, and then, eluding her
encouraging stare, gave her a twenty-franc note and took a
taxi to his hotel.

II

He woke upon a fine fall day—football weather.

The depression of yesterday was gone and he liked the
people on the streets. At noon he sat opposite Honoria at
the Grand Vatel, the only restaurant he could think of not
reminiscent of champagne dinners and long luncheons
that began at two and ended in a blurred and vague
twilight.

"Now, how about vegetables? Oughtn't you to have
some vegetables?"

"Well, yes."

"Here's *épinards* and *chou-fleur* and carrots and
haricots."

"I'd like *choux-fleurs.*"

"Wouldn't you like to have two vegetables?"

"I usually only have one at lunch."

The waiter was pretending to be inordinately fond of
children. *"Qu'elle est mignonne la petite? Elle parle exact-*
ment comme une francaise."

"How about dessert? Shall we wait and see?"

The waiter disappeared. Honoria looked at him expectantly.

"What are we going to do?"

"First we're going to that toy store in the Rue St.
Honoré and buy you anything you like. And then we're
going to the vaudeville at the Empire."

She hesitated. "I like it about the vaudeville, but not
the toy store."

"Why not?"

"Well, you brought me this doll." She had it with her.
"And I've got lots of things. And we're not rich anymore,
are we?"

"We never were. But today you are to have anything
you want."

"All right," she agreed resignedly.

He had always been fond of her, but when there had
been her mother and a French nurse he had been inclined
to be strict; now he extended himself, reached out for a
new tolerance; he must be both parents to her and not shut
any of her out of communication.

"I want to get to know you," he said gravely. "First let
me introduce myself. My name is Charles J. Wales, of
Prague."

"Oh, daddy!" her voice cracked with laughter.

"And who are you, please?" he persisted, and she
accepted a role immediately: "Honoria Wales, Rue Palatine, Paris."

"Married or single?"

"No, not married. Single."

He indicated the doll. "But I see you have a child, madame."

Unwilling to disinherit it, she took it to her heart and thought quickly: "Yes, I've been married, but I'm not married now. My husband is dead."

He went on quickly, "And the child's name?"

"Simone. That's after my best friend at school."

"I'm very pleased that you're doing so well at school."

"I'm third this month," she boasted. "Elsie"–that was her cousin–"is only about eighteenth, and Richard is about at the bottom."

"You like Richard and Elsie, don't you?"

"Oh, yes. I like Richard quite well and I like her all right."

Cautiously and casually he asked: "And Aunt Marion and Uncle Lincoln–which do you like best?"

"Oh, Uncle Lincoln, I guess."

He was increasingly aware of her presence. As they came in, a murmur of "What an adorable child" followed them, and now the people at the next table bent all their silences upon her, staring as if she were something no more conscious than a flower.

"Why don't I live with you?" she asked suddenly. "Because mamma's dead?"

"You must stay here and learn more French. It would have been hard for daddy to take care of you so well."

"I don't really need much taking care of anymore. I do everything for myself."

Going out of the restaurant, a man and a woman unexpectedly hailed him!

"Well, the old Wales!"

"Hello there, Lorraine. . . . Dunc."

Sudden ghosts out of the past: Duncan Schaeffer, a friend from college. Lorraine Quarrles, a lovely, pale blonde of thirty; one of a crowd who had helped them make months into days in the lavish times of two years ago.

"My husband couldn't come this year," she said, in answer to his question. "We're poor as hell. So he gave me two hundred a month and told me I could do my worst on that. . . . This your little girl?"

"What about sitting down?" Duncan asked.

"Can't do it." He was glad for an excuse. As always, he felt Lorraine's passionate, provocative attraction, but his own rhythm was different now.

"Well, how about dinner?" she asked.

"I'm not free. Give me your address and let me call you."

"Charlie, I believe you're sober," she said judicially. "I honestly believe he's sober, Dunc. Pinch him and see if he's sober."

Charlie indicated Honoria with his head. They both laughed.

"What's your address?" said Duncan skeptically.

He hesitated, unwilling to give the name of his hotel.

"I'm not settled yet. I'd better call you. We're going to see the vaudeville at the Empire."

"There! That's what I want to do," Lorraine said. "I want to see some clowns and acrobats and jugglers. That's just what we'll do, Dunc."

"We've got to do an errand first," said Charlie. "Perhaps we'll see you there."

"All right, you snob. . . . Good-bye, beautiful little girl."

"Good-bye." Honoria bobbed politely.

Somehow, an unpleasant encounter, Charlie thought. They liked him because he was functioning, because he was serious; they wanted to see him, because he was stronger than they were now, because they wanted to draw a certain sustenance from his strength.

At the Empire, Honoria proudly refused to sit upon her father's folded coat. She was already an individual with a code of her own, and Charlie was more and more absorbed by the desire of putting a little of himself into her before she crystallized utterly. It was hopeless to try to know her in so short a time.

Between acts they came upon Duncan and Lorraine in the lobby where the band was playing.

"Have a drink?"

"All right, but not up at the bar. We'll take a table."

"The perfect father."

Listening abstractedly to Lorraine, Charlie watched Honoria's eyes leave them all, and he followed them wistfully about the room, wondering what they saw. He met them and she smiled.

"I liked that lemonade," she said.

What had she said? What had he expected? Going home in a taxi afterward, he pulled her over until her head rested against his chest.

"Darling, do you ever think about your mother?"

"Yes, sometimes," she answered vaguely.

"I don't want you to forget her. Have you got a picture of her?"

"Yes, I think so. Anyhow, Aunt Marion has. Why don't you want me to forget her?"

"She loved you very much."

"I loved her too."

They were silent for a moment.

"Daddy, I want to come and live with you," she said suddenly.

His heart leaped; he had wanted it to come like this.

"Aren't you perfectly happy?"

"Yes, but I love you better than anybody. And you love me better than anybody, don't you, now that mummy's dead?"

"Of course I do. But you won't always like me best, honey. You'll grow up and meet somebody your own age and go marry him and forget you ever had a daddy."

"Yes, that's true," she agreed tranquilly.

He didn't go in. He was coming back at nine o'clock and he wanted to keep himself fresh and new for the thing he must say then.

"When you're safe inside, just show yourself in that window."

Hollywood was afraid of her, though she didn't need good direction or acting advice. So her success was her own.

"All right. Good-bye, dads, dads, dads, dads."

He waited in the dark street until she appeared, all warm and glowing, in the window above and kissed her fingers out into the night.

III

They were waiting. Marion sat behind empty coffee cups in a dignified black dinner dress that just faintly suggested mourning. Lincoln was walking up and down with the animation of one who had already been talking. They were as anxious as he was to get into the question. He opened it almost immediately:

"I suppose you know what I want to see you about—why I really came to Paris."

Marion fiddled with the glass grapes on her necklace and frowned.

"I'm awfully anxious to have a home," he continued. "And I'm awfully anxious to have Honoria in it. I appreciate your taking in Honoria for her mother's sake, but things have changed now"—he hesitated and then continued strongly—"changed radically with me, and I want to ask you to reconsider the matter. It would be silly for me to deny that about two years ago I was acting badly——"

Marion looked up at him with hard eyes.

"——but all that's over. As I told you, I haven't had more than a drink a day for over a year, and I take that drink deliberately, so that the idea of alcohol won't get too big in my imagination. You see the idea?"

"No," said Marion succinctly.

"It's a sort of stunt I set myself. It keeps the matter in proportion."

"I get you," said Lincoln. "You don't want to admit it's got any attraction for you."

"Something like that. Sometimes I forget and don't take it. But I try to take it. Anyhow, I couldn't afford to drink in my position. The people I represent are more than satisfied with what I've done, and I'm bringing my sister over from Burlington to keep house for me, and I want awfully to have Honoria too. You know that even when her mother and I weren't getting along well I never let anything that happened touch Honoria. I know she's fond of me and I know I'm able to take care of her and—well, there you are. How do you feel about it?"

He knew that now he would have to take a beating. It would last an hour or two hours, and it would be difficult, but if he modulated his inevitable resentment to the chastened attitude of the reformed sinner, he might win his point in the end. "Keep your temper," he told himself. "You don't want to be justified. You want Honoria."

Lincoln spoke first: "We've been talking it over ever since we got your letter last month. We're happy to have Honoria here. She's a dear little thing, and we're glad to be able to help her, but of course that isn't the question——"

Marion interrupted suddenly. "How long are you going to stay sober, Charlie?" she asked.

"Permanently, I hope."

"How can anybody count on that?"

"You know I never did drink heavily until I gave up business and came over here with nothing to do. Then Helen and I began to run around with——"

"Please leave Helen out of it. I can't bear to hear you talk about her like that."

He stared at her grimly; he had never been certain how fond of each other the sisters were in life.

"My drinking only lasted about a year and a half—from the time we came over until I—collapsed."

"It was time enough."

"It was time enough," he agreed.

"My duty is entirely to Helen," she said. "I try to think what she would have wanted me to do. Frankly, from the night you did that terrible thing you haven't really existed for me. I can't help that. She was my sister."

"Yes."

"When she was dying she asked me to look out for Honoria. If you hadn't been in a sanitarium then, it might have helped matters."

He had no answer.

"I'll never in my life be able to forget the morning when Helen knocked at my door, soaked to the skin and shivering, and said you'd locked her out."

Charlie gripped the sides of the chair. This was more difficult than he expected; he wanted to launch out into a long expostulation and explanation, but he only said: "The night I locked her out——" and she interrupted, "I don't feel up to going over that again."

After a moment's silence Lincoln said: "We're getting off the subject. You want Marion to set aside her legal guardianship and give you Honoria. I think the main point for her is whether she has confidence in you or not."

"I don't blame Marion," Charlie said slowly, "but I think she can have entire confidence in me. I had a good record up to three years ago. Of course, it's within human possibilities I might go wrong any time. But if we wait much longer I'll lose Honoria's childhood and my chance for a home. I'll simply lose her, don't you see?"

"Yes, I see," said Lincoln.

"Why didn't you think of all this before?" Marion asked.

"I suppose I did, from time to time, but Helen and I were getting along badly. When I consented to the guardianship, I was flat on my back in a sanitarium and the market had cleaned me out of every sou. I knew I'd acted badly, and I thought if it would bring any peace to Helen, I'd agree to anything. But now it's different. I'm well, I'm functioning, I'm behaving damn well, so far as——"

"Please don't swear at me," Marion said.

He looked at her, startled. With each remark the force of her dislike became more and more apparent. She had built up all her fear of life into one wall and faced it toward him. This trivial reproof was possibly the result of some trouble with the cook several hours before. Charlie became increasingly alarmed at leaving Honoria in this atmosphere of hostility against himself; sooner or later it would come out, in a word here, a shake of the head there, and some of that distrust would be irrevocably implanted in Honoria. But he pulled his temper down out of his face and shut it up inside him; he had won a point, for Lincoln realized the absurdity of Marion's remark and asked her lightly since when she had objected to the word "damn."

"Another thing," Charlie said: "I'm able to give her certain advantages now. I'm going to take a French governess to Prague with me. I've got a lease on a new apartment——"

He stopped, realizing that he was blundering. They couldn't be expected to accept with equanimity the fact that his income was again twice as large as their own.

"I suppose you can give her more luxuries than we can," said Marion. "When you were throwing away money we were living along watching every ten francs. . . . I suppose you'll start doing it again."

"Oh, no," he said. "I've learned. I worked hard for ten years, you know—until I got lucky in the market, like so many people. Terribly lucky. It didn't seem any use working anymore, so I quit. It won't happen again."

There was a long silence. All of them felt their nerves straining, and for the first time in a year Charlie wanted a drink. He was sure now that Lincoln Peters wanted him to have his child.

Marion shuddered suddenly; part of her saw that Charlie's feet were planted on the earth now, and her own maternal feeling recognized the naturalness of his desire; but she had lived for a long time with a prejudice—a prejudice founded on a curious disbelief in her sister's happiness, and which, in the shock of one terrible night, had turned to hatred for him. It had all happened at a point in her life where the discouragement of ill health and adverse circumstances made it necessary for her to believe in tangible villainy and a tangible villain.

"I can't help what I think!" she cried out suddenly. "How much you were responsible for Helen's death, I don't know. It's something you'll have to square with your own conscience."

An electric current of agony surged through him; for a moment he was almost on his feet, an unuttered sound echoing in his throat. He hung on to himself for a moment, another moment.

"Hold on there," said Lincoln uncomfortably. "I never thought you were responsible for that."

"Helen died of heart trouble," Charlie said dully.

"Yes, heart trouble." Marion spoke as if the phrase had another meaning for her.

Then, in the flatness that followed her outburst, she saw him plainly and she knew he had somehow arrived at control over the situation. Glancing at her husband, she found no help from him, and as abruptly as if it were a matter of no importance, she threw up the sponge.

"Do what you like!" she cried, springing up from her chair. "She's your child. I'm not the person to stand in your way. I think if it were my child I'd rather see her——" She managed to check herself. "You two decide it. I can't stand this. I'm sick. I'm going to bed."

She hurried from the room; after a moment Lincoln said:

"This has been a hard day for her. You know how strongly she feels——" His voice was almost apologetic: "When a woman gets an idea in her head."

"Of course."

"It's going to be all right. I think she sees now that you—can provide for the child, and so we can't very well stand in your way or Honoria's way."

"Thank you, Lincoln."

"I'd better go along and see how she is."

"I'm going."

He was still trembling when he reached the street, but a walk down the Rue Bonaparte to the quais set him up, and as he crossed the Seine, dotted with many cold moons, he felt exultant. But back in his room he couldn't sleep. The image of Helen haunted him. Helen whom he had loved so until they had senselessly begun to abuse each other's love and tear it into shreds. On that terrible February night that Marion remembered so vividly, a slow quarrel that had gone on for hours. There was a scene at the Florida, and then he attempted to take her home, and then Helen kissed Ted Wilder at a table, and what she had hysterically said. Charlie's departure and, on his arrival home, his turning the key in the lock in wild anger. How could he know she would arrive an hour later alone, that there would be a snowstorm in which she wandered about in slippers for an hour, too confused to find a taxi? Then the aftermath, her escaping pneumonia by a miracle, and all the attendant horror. They were "reconciled," but that was the beginning of the end, and Marion, who had seen

Fitzgerald wrote of a lost generation, brilliant, beautiful expatriates who he said went to Paris when they died (if they weren't already there).

with her own eyes and who imagined it to be one of many scenes from her sister's martyrdom, never forgot.

Going over it again brought Helen nearer, and in the white, soft light that steals upon half sleep near morning he found himself talking to her again. She said that he was perfectly right about Honoria and that she wanted Honoria to be with him. She said she was glad he was being good and doing better. She said a lot of other things—very friendly things—but she was in a swing in a white dress, and swinging faster and faster all the time, so that at the end he could not hear clearly all that she said.

IV

He woke up feeling happy. The door of the world was open again. He made plans, vistas, futures for Honoria and himself, but suddenly he grew sad, remembering all the plans he and Helen had made. She had not planned to die. The present was the thing—work to do and someone to love. But not to love too much, for Charlie had read in D. H. Lawrence about the injury that a father can do to a daughter or a mother to a son by attaching them too closely. Afterward, out in the world, the child would seek in the marriage partner the same blind, unselfish tenderness and, failing in all human probability to find it, develop a grudge against love and life.

It was another bright, crisp day. He called Lincoln Peters at the bank where he worked and asked if he could count on taking Honoria when he left for Prague. Lincoln agreed that there was no reason for delay. One thing—the legal guardianship. Marion wanted to retain that a while longer. She was upset by the whole matter, and it would oil things if she felt that the situation was still in her control for another year. Charlie agreed, wanting only the tangible, visible child.

Then the question of a governess. Charlie sat in a gloomy agency and talked to a buxom Breton peasant whom he knew he couldn't endure. There were others whom he could see tomorrow.

He lunched with Lincoln Peters at the Griffon, trying to keep down his exultation.

"There's nothing quite like your own child," Lincoln said. "But you understand how Marion feels too."

"She's forgotten how hard I worked for seven years there," Charlie said. "She just remembers one night."

"There's another thing." Lincoln hesitated. "While you and Helen were tearing around Europe throwing money away, we were just getting along. I didn't touch any of the prosperity because I never got ahead enough to carry anything but my insurance. I think Marion felt there was some kind of injustice in it—you not even working and getting richer and richer."

"It went just as quick as it came," said Charlie.

"A lot did. And a lot of it stayed in the hands of *chasseurs* and saxophone players and maîtres d'hôtel—well, the big party's over now. I just said that to explain Marion's feelings about those crazy years. If you drop in about six o'clock tonight before Marion's too tired, we'll settle the details on the spot."

Back at his hotel, Charlie took from his pocket a *pneumatique* that Lincoln had given him at luncheon. It had been redirected by Paul from the hotel bar.

Dear Charlie: You were so strange when we saw you the other day that I wondered if I did something to offend you. If so, I'm not conscious of it. In fact, I have thought about you too much for the last year, and it's always been in the back of my mind that I might see you if I came over here. We did have such good times that crazy spring, like the night you and I stole the butcher's tricycle, and the time we tried to call on the president and you had the old derby and the wire cane. Everybody seems so old lately, but I don't feel old a bit. Couldn't we get together sometime today for old times' sake? I've got a vile hangover for the moment, but will be feeling better this afternoon and will look for you about five at the bar.

Always devotedly,
LORRAINE.

His first feeling was one of awe that he had actually, in his mature years, stolen a tricycle and pedaled Lorraine all over the Etoile between the small hours and dawn. In retrospect it was a nightmare. Locking out Helen didn't fit in with any other act of his life, but the tricycle incident did—it was one of many. How many weeks or months of dissipation to arrive at that condition of utter irresponsibility?

He tried to picture how Lorraine had appeared to him then—very attractive; so much so that Helen had been jealous. Yesterday, in the restaurant, she had seemed trite, blurred, worn away. He emphatically did not want to see her, and he was glad no one knew at what hotel he was staying. It was a relief to think of Honoria, to think of Sundays spent with her and of saying good morning to her and of knowing she was there in his house at night, breathing quietly in the darkness.

At five he took a taxi and bought presents for all the Peters—a piquant cloth doll, a box of Roman soldiers, flowers for Marion, big linen handkerchiefs for Lincoln.

He saw, when he arrived in the apartment, that Marion had accepted the inevitable. She greeted him now as though he were a recalcitrant member of the family, rather than a menacing outsider. Honoria had been told she was going, and Charlie was glad to see that her tact was sufficient to conceal her excessive happiness. Only on his lap did she whisper her delight and the question "When?" before she slipped away.

He and Marion were alone for a minute in the room, and on an impulse he spoke out boldly:

"Family quarrels are bitter things. They don't go according to my rules. They're not like aches or wounds; they're more like splits in the skin that won't heal because there's not enough material. I wish you and I could be on better terms."

"Some things are hard to forget," she answered. "It's a question of confidence. If you behave yourself in the future I won't have any criticism of you." There was no answer to this comment, and presently, after some silence,

Freckle-faced Van Johnson with Taylor in **The Last Time I Saw Paris**. *Victorious over cancer and still youngish, Johnson is present-day king of the dinner theater circuit.*

she asked, "When do you propose to take her?"

"As soon as I can get a governess. I hoped the day after tomorrow."

"That's impossible. I've got to get her things in shape. Not before Saturday."

He yielded. Coming back into the room, Lincoln offered him a drink.

"I'll take my daily whisky," he said.

It was warm here, it was a home, people together by a fire. The children felt very safe and important; the mother and father were serious, watchful. They had things to do for the children more important than his visit here. A spoonful of medicine was, after all, more important than the strained relations between Marion and himself. They were not dull people, but they were very much in the grip of life and circumstances, and their gestures as they turned in a cramped space lacked largeness and grace. He wondered if he couldn't do something to get Lincoln out of that rut at the bank.

There was a long peal at the doorbell; the maid crossed the room and went down the corridor. The door opened upon another long ring, and then voices, and the three in the salon looked up expectantly; Richard moved to bring the corridor within his range of vision, and Marion rose. Then the maid came along the corridor, closely followed by the voices, which developed under the light into Duncan Schaeffer and Lorraine Quarrles.

They were gay, they were hilarious, they were roaring with laughter. For a moment Charlie was astounded; then he realized they had got the address he had left at the bar.

"Ah-h-h!" Duncan wagged his finger roguishly at Charlie. "Ah-h-h!"

They both slid down into another cascade of laughter. Anxious and at a loss, Charlie shook hands with them quickly and presented them to Lincoln and Marion. Marion nodded, scarcely speaking. She had drawn back a step toward the fire; her little girl stood beside her, and Marion put an arm about her shoulder.

With growing annoyance at the intrusion, Charlie waited for them to explain themselves. After some concentration Duncan said:

"We came to take you to dinner. Lorraine and I insist that all this shi-shi, cagy business got to stop."

Charlie came closer to them, as if to force them backward down the corridor.

"Sorry, but I can't. Tell me where you'll be and we'll call you in half an hour."

This made no impression. Lorraine sat down suddenly on the side of a chair, and focusing her eyes on Richard, cried, "Oh, what a nice little boy! Come here, little boy." Richard glanced at his mother, but did not move. With a perceptible shrug of her shoulders, Lorraine turned back to Charlie:

"Come on out to dinner. Be yourself, Charlie. Come on."

"How about a little drink?" said Duncan to the room at large.

Lincoln Peters had been somewhat uneasily occupying himself by swinging Honoria from side to side with her feet off the ground.

"I'm sorry, but there isn't a thing in the house," he said. "We just this minute emptied the only bottle."

"All the more reason for coming to dinner," Lorraine

assured Charlie. "You will come, won't you?"

"I can't," said Charlie almost sharply. "You two go have dinner and I'll phone you."

"Oh, you will, will you?" Her voice became suddenly unpleasant. "All right, we'll go along. But I remember, when you used to hammer on my door, I used to be enough of a good sport to give you a drink. Come on, Dunc."

Still in slow motion, with blurred, angry faces, with uncertain feet, they retired along the corridor.

"Good night," Charlie said.

"Good night!" responded Lorraine emphatically.

When he went back into the salon Marion had not moved, only now her son was standing in the circle of her other arm. Lincoln was still swinging Honoria back and forth like a pendulum from side to side.

"What an outrage!" Charlie broke out. "What an absolute outrage!"

Neither of them answered. Charlie dropped into an armchair, picked up his drink, set it down again and said:

"People I haven't seen for two years having the colossal nerve——"

He broke off. Marion had made the sound "Oh!" in one swift, furious breath, turned her body from him with a jerk and left the room.

Lincoln set down Honoria carefully.

"You children go in and start your soup," he said, and when they obeyed, he said to Charlie:

"Marion's not well and she can't stand shocks. That kind of people make her really physically sick."

"I didn't tell them to come here. They wormed this address out of Paul at the bar. They deliberately——"

"Well, it's too bad. It doesn't help matters. Excuse me a minute."

Left alone, Charlie sat tense in his chair. In the next room he could hear the children eating, talking in monosyllables, already oblivious of the scene among their elders. He heard a murmur of conversation from a farther room and then the ticking bell of a phone picked up, and in a panic he moved to the other side of the room and out of earshot.

In a minute Lincoln came back. "Look here, Charlie. I think we'd better call off dinner for tonight. Marion's in bad shape."

"Is she angry with me?"

"Sort of," he said, almost roughly. "She's not strong and ——"

"You mean she's changed her mind about Honoria?"

"She's pretty bitter right now. I don't know. You phone me at the bank tomorrow."

"I wish you'd explain to her I never dreamed these people would come here. I'm just as sore as you are."

"I couldn't explain anything to her now."

Charlie got up. He took his coat and hat and started down the corridor. Then he opened the door of the dining room and said in a strange voice, "Good night, children."

Honoria rose and ran around the table to hug him.

"Good night, sweetheart," he said vaguely, and then trying to make his voice more tender, trying to conciliate something, "Good night, dear children."

Charlie went directly to the bar with the furious idea of finding Lorraine and Duncan, but they were not there, and he realized that in any case there was nothing he could do. He had not touched his drink at the Peters', and now he ordered a whisky-and-soda. Paul came over to say hello.

"It's a great change," he said sadly. "We do about half the business we did. So many fellows I hear about back in the States lost everything, maybe not in the first crash, but then in the second, and now when everything keeps going down. Your friend George Hardt lost every cent, I hear. Are you back in the States?"

"No, I'm in business in Prague."

"I heard that you lost a lot in the crash."

"I did," and he added grimly, "but I lost everything I wanted in the boom."

"Selling short."

"Something like that."

Again the memory of those days swept over him like a nightmare—the people they had met traveling; then people who couldn't add a row of figures or speak a coherent sentence. The little man Helen had consented to dance with at the ship's party, who had insulted her ten feet from the table; the human mosaic of pearls who sat behind them at the Russian ballet and, when the curtain rose on a scene, remarked to her companion: "Luffly; just luffly. Zomebody ought to baint a bicture of it." Men who locked their wives out in the snow, because the snow of twenty-nine wasn't real snow. If you didn't want it to be snow, you just paid some money.

He went to the phone and called the Peters' apartment; Lincoln himself answered.

"I called up because, as you can imagine, this thing is on my mind. Has Marion said anything definite?"

"Marion's sick," Lincoln answered shortly. "I know this thing isn't altogether your fault, but I can't have her go to pieces about this. I'm afraid we'll have to let it slide for six months; I can't take the chance of working her up to this state again."

"I see."

"I'm sorry, Charlie."

He went back to his table. His whisky glass was empty, but he shook his head when Alix looked at it questioningly. There wasn't much he could do now except send Honoria some things; he would send her a lot of things tomorrow. He thought rather angrily that that was just money—he had given so many people money.

"No, no more," he said to another waiter. "What do I owe you?"

He would come back someday; they couldn't make him pay forever. But he wanted his child, and nothing was much good now, beside that fact. He wasn't young anymore, with a lot of nice thoughts and dreams to have by himself. He was absolutely sure Helen wouldn't have wanted him to be so alone.

(1931)

Grizzly Adams
by Horace S. Mazet

In the spring of 1853 occurred the incident which determined James Capen Adams' future and the name by which he was to grow famous. His brother William, fresh from the Northern California gold mines and rich, discovered his retreat and signed a contract with him in which he agreed to capture wild beasts for shipment to the East Coast, profits to be split between them. Grizzly, long having wished to visit the unknown Northwest, now had an objective in view.

Never hunting for sport, and killing only for food or to effect the capture of fiercely guarded young, the party

Dan Haggerty in **The Life and Times of Grizzly Adams,** *a saccharinized version of the biography in the* **Post.**

found thrill-packed adventures in combat with wolves, deer, elk, buffaloes and, of course, more bears.

In one such fight, Adams struggled hand to paw with two small bears, resulting in considerable damage to his hands. Spartan medical treatment of simple cold-water compresses, and his husky physique, soon proved effective. Wounds gave Adams small concern—indeed, his methods seemed to invite them. By first trying for a kill with his muzzle-loader, he saved time and trouble. But if a bear was merely wounded, Adams showed no hesitation in closing with pistol and drawn bowie knife. The contest invariably ended with a dead bear and a scratched, bitten and cuffed hunter. *(1946)*

Murder in the Calais Coach

by Agatha Christie

"Had you an affection for your employer, Masterman?"

Masterman's face became, if possible, even more inexpressive than it was normally.

"I should hardly like to say that, sir. He was a generous employer."

"But you didn't like him?"

"Shall we put it that I don't care very much for Americans, sir?"

"Have you ever been in America?"

"No, sir."

"Do you remember reading in the paper of the Armstrong kidnaping case?"

A little color came into the man's cheeks.

"Yes, indeed, sir. A little girl, wasn't it? A very shocking affair."

"Did you know that your employer, Mr. Ratchett, was the principal instigator in that affair?"

"No, indeed, sir." The valet's tone held positive warmth and feeling for the first time. "I can hardly believe it, sir."

"Nevertheless, it is true. . . . Now, to pass to your own movements last night. A matter of routine, you understand. What did you do after leaving your master?"

"I told Mr. MacQueen, sir, that the master wanted him. Then I went to my own compartment and read."

"Your compartment was——"

"The end second-class one, sir. Next to the dining car."

Poirot was looking at his plan.

"I see—and you had which berth?"

"The lower one, sir."

"That is No. 4?"

"Yes, sir."

"Is there anyone in with you?"

"Yes, sir. A big Italian fellow."

"Does he speak English?"

"Well, a kind of English, sir." The valet's tone was deprecating. "He's been in America—Chicago, I understand."

"Do you and he talk together much?"

"No, sir. I prefer to read."

Poirot smiled. He could visualize the scene—the large, voluble Italian, and the snub direct administered by the gentleman's gentleman in the compartment.

"And what, may I ask, are you reading?"

"At present, sir, I am reading *Love's Captive* by Mrs. Arabella Richardson."

"A good story?"

"I find it highly enjoyable, sir. . . ."

. . . .

"You have given us most interesting and valuable evidence," said Poirot soothingly. "Now, may I ask you a few questions?"

"Why, willingly."

"How was it, since you were nervous of this man Ratchett, that you hadn't already bolted the door between the compartments?"

"I had," returned Mrs. Hubbard promptly.

"Oh, you had?"

"Well, as a matter of fact I asked that Swedish creature—a pleasant soul—if it was bolted, and she said it was."

"How was it you couldn't see for yourself?"

"Because I was in bed and my sponge bag was hanging on the door handle."

"What time was it when you asked her to do this?"

"Now let me think. It must have been round about half-past ten or a quarter to eleven. She'd come along to see if I'd got an aspirin. I told her where to find it, and she got it out of my grip."

"You yourself were in bed?"

"Yes."

Suddenly she laughed.

"Poor soul, she was in quite a taking. You see, she'd opened the door of the next compartment by mistake."

"Mr. Ratchett's?"

"Yes. You know how difficult it is as you come along the train and all the doors are shut. She opened his by mistake. She was very distressed about it. He'd laughed, it seemed, and I fancy he may have said something not quite nice. Poor thing, she was all in a flutter. 'Oh, I make mistake,' she said. 'I ashamed make mistake. Not nice man,' she said. 'He say, "You too old." ' "

Doctor Constantine sniggered and Mrs. Hubbard immediately froze him with a glance.

The 1974 movie version called **Murder on the Orient Express** *starred Albert Finney as the dapper Poirot, seen here confronting passengers that include Lauren Bacall and Ingrid Bergman. The real train ended service in 1977.*

. . . .

M. Bouc gave directions to the dining-car attendant, and presently the lady with the yellowish-gray bun of hair and the long, mild, sheeplike face was ushered in. She peered shortsightedly at Poirot through her glasses, but was quite calm.

It transpired that she understood and spoke French, so the conversation took place in that language. Poirot first asked her the questions to which he already knew the answers—her name, age, and address. He then asked her her occupation.

She was, she told him, matron in a missionary school near Stamboul. She was a trained nurse.

"You know, of course, of what took place last night, mademoiselle?"

"Naturally. It is very dreadful. And the American lady tells me that the murderer was actually in her compartment."

"I hear, mademoiselle, that you were the last person to see the murdered man alive?"

"I do not know. It may be so. I opened the door of his compartment by mistake. I was much ashamed. It was a most awkward mistake."

"You actually saw him?"

"Yes. He was reading a book. I apologized quickly and withdrew."

"Did he say anything to you?"

A slight flush showed on the worthy lady's cheek.

"He laughed and said a few words. I—I did not quite

catch them. I was unable to hear well."

"And what did you do after that, mademoiselle?" asked Poirot, passing from the subject tactfully.

"I went in to the American lady—Mrs. Hubbard. I asked her for some aspirin and she gave it to me."

"Did she ask you whether the door between her compartment and that of Mr. Ratchett was bolted?"

"Yes."

"And was it?"

"Yes."

"And after that?"

"After that I go back to my own compartment, I take the aspirin and lie down."

"What time was all this?"

"When I got into bed, it was five minutes to eleven, because I look at my watch before I wind it up."

"Did you go to sleep quickly?"

"Not very quickly. My head got better, but I lay awake some time."

"Had the train come to a stop before you went to sleep?"

"I do not think so. We stopped, I think, at a station, just as I was getting drowsy."

"That would be Vinkovci. Now, your compartment, mademoiselle, is this one?" He indicated it on the plan.

"That is so, yes."

"You had the upper or the lower berth?"

"The lower berth, No. 10."

"And you had a companion?"

"Yes, a young English lady. Very nice, very amiable. She had traveled from Bagdad."

"After the train left Vinkovci, did she leave the compartment?"

"No, I am sure she did not."

"Why are you sure, if you were asleep?"

"I sleep very lightly. I am used to waking at a sound. I am sure if she had come down from the berth above, I should have awakened."

"Did you yourself leave the compartment?"

"Not until this morning."

"Have you a scarlet-silk kimono, mademoiselle?"

"No, indeed. I have a good, comfortable dressing gown of woolen material."

. . . .

Her small toadlike face looked even yellower than the day before. She was certainly ugly, and yet, like the toad, she had eyes like jewels, dark and imperious, revealing latent energy and an intellectual force that could be felt at once.

Her voice was deep, very distinct, with a slight grating quality in it.

She cut short a flowery phrase of apology from M. Bouc:

"You need not offer apologies, messieurs. I understand a murder has taken place. Naturally, you must interview all the passengers. I shall be glad to give you all the assistance in my power."

"You are most amiable, madame," said Poirot.

"Not at all. It is a duty. What do you wish to know?"

"Your full Christian names and address, madame. Perhaps you would prefer to write them yourself?"

Poirot proffered a sheet of paper and pencil, but the princess waved them aside.

"You can write it," she said. "There is nothing difficult: Natasha Sonia Dragiloff, Avenue Kleber, Paris."

"You are traveling home from Constantinople, madame?"

"Yes. I have been staying at the Austrian Embassy. My maid is with me."

"Would you be so good as to give me a brief account of your movements last night from dinner onwards?"

"Willingly. I directed the conductor to make up my berth whilst I was in the dining car. I retired to bed immediately after dinner. I read until the hour of eleven, when I turned out my light. I was unable to sleep, owing to certain rheumatic pains from which I suffer. At about a quarter to one I rang for my maid. She massaged me and then read aloud till I felt sleepy. I cannot say exactly when she left me. It may have been half an hour, it may have been later."

"The train had stopped then?"

"The train had stopped."

"You heard nothing—nothing unusual—during the time, madame?"

"I heard nothing unusual."

"What is your maid's name?"

"Hildegarde Schmidt."

"She has been with you long?"

"Fifteen years."

"You consider her to be trustworthy?"

"Absolutely. Her people come from an estate of my late husband's in Germany."

"You have been in America, I presume, madame?"

The abrupt change of subject made the old lady raise her eyebrows.

"Many times."

"Were you at any time acquainted with a family of the name of Armstrong—a family in which a tragedy occurred?"

With some emotion in her voice the old lady said:

"You speak of friends of mine, monsieur."

"You knew Doctor Armstrong well, then?"

"I knew him slightly, but his wife, Sonia Armstrong, was my goddaughter. I was on terms of friendship with her mother, the actress, Linda Arden. Linda Arden was a great genius, one of the greatest tragic actresses in the world. As Lady Macbeth, as Magda, there was no one to touch her. I was not only an admirer of her art, I was a personal friend."

"She is dead?"

"No, no, she is alive, but she lives in complete retirement. Her health is very delicate; she has to lie on a sofa most of the time."

"There was, I think, a second daughter?"

"Yes, much younger than Mrs. Armstrong."

"And she is alive?"

"Certainly."

"Where is she?"

The old woman bent an acute glance at him.

"I must ask you the reason of these questions. What have they to do with the matter in hand—the murder on this train?"

"They are connected in this way, madame: The man who was murdered was the man responsible for the kidnaping and murder of Mrs. Armstrong's child."

"Ah!"

The straight brows drew together. Princess Dragiloff drew herself a little more erect.

"In my view, then, this murder is an entirely admirable happening! You will pardon my slightly biased point of view."

. . . .

"Have you ever been in America, Colonel Arbuthnot?"

"Never. Don't want to go."

"Did you ever know a Doctor Armstrong?"

"Armstrong—Armstrong—I've known two or three Armstrongs."

"I mean the Doctor Armstrong who married an American wife and whose daughter was kidnaped and killed."

"Ah, yes, I remember reading about that—shocking affair. I don't think I actually ever came across the fellow, though, of course, I knew of him. Toby Armstrong. Nice fellow. Everybody liked him. He had a very distinguished career. Got the V.C."

"The man who was killed last night was the man responsible for the murder of Dr. Armstrong's child."

Arbuthnot's face grew rather grim.

"Then, in my opinion, the swine deserved what he got. Though I would have preferred to have seen him properly hanged, or electrocuted, I suppose, over there."

"In fact, Colonel Arbuthnot, you prefer law and order to private vengeance?"

"Well, you can't go about having blood feuds and stabbing each other like Corsicans or the mafia," said the colonel. "Say what you like, trial by jury is a sound system."

Poirot looked at him thoughtfully for a minute or two.

"Yes," he said. "I am sure that would be your view."

. . . .

"You are Cyrus Bethman Hardman, United States subject, forty-one years of age, traveling salesman for typewriting ribbons?"

"O.K. That's me."

"You are traveling from Stamboul to Paris?"

"That's so."

"Reason?"

"Business."

"Do you always travel first class, Mr. Hardman?"

"Yes, sir. The firm pays my traveling expenses."

He winked.

"Now, Mr. Hardman, we come to the events of last night."

The American nodded.

"What can you tell us about the matter?"

"Exactly nothing at all."

"Ah, that is a pity. Perhaps, Mr. Hardman, you will tell us exactly what you did last night from dinner onwards?"

For the first time the American did not seem ready with his reply. At last he said:

"Excuse me, gentlemen, but just who are you? Put me wise."

"This is M. Bouc, a director of the Compagnie des Wagons-Lits. This gentleman is the doctor who examined the body."

"And you yourself?"

"I am Hercule Poirot. I am engaged by the company to investigate this matter."

"I've heard of you," said Mr. Hardman. He reflected a minute or two longer. "Guess I'd better come clean."

"It will certainly be advisable for you to tell us all you know," said Poirot dryly.

"You'd have said a mouthful if there was anything I did know. But I don't. I know nothing at all—just as I said. But I ought to know something. That's what makes me sore. I ought to."

"Please explain, Mr. Hardman."

Mr. Hardman sighed and dived into a pocket. At the same time his whole personality seemed to undergo a change. He became less of a stage character and more of a real person. The resonant, nasal tones of his voice became modified.

British-born Albert Finney was nominated for an Oscar for his portrayal of Agatha Christie's suave super-sleuth; also for his role in Tom Jones.

"That passport's a bit of bluff," he said. "That's who I really am."

Poirot scrutinized the card flipped across to him. M. Bouc peered over his shoulder.

MR. CYRUS B. HARDMAN
MCNEIL'S DETECTIVE AGENCY
NEW YORK

Poirot knew the name. It was one of the best-known and most reputable private detective agencies in New York.

"Now, Mr. Hardman," he said, "let us hear the meaning of this."

"Sure. Things came about this way: I'd come over to Europe trailing a couple of crooks—nothing to do with this business. The chase ended in Stamboul. I wired the chief and got his instructions to return, and I would have been making my tracks back to little old New York, when I got this."

He pushed across a letter. The heading at the top was the Tokatlian Hotel.

Dear Sir: You have been pointed out to me as an operative of the McNeil Detective Agency. Kindly report to my suite at four o'clock this afternoon.

It was signed "S. E. Ratchett." *(1933)*

Fantastic Voyage
by Isaac Asimov

The 1966 movie featured Raquel Welch (far left) and Donald Pleasance (second from right), has become late-night T.V. standard.

Isaac Asimov wrote the novel appearing in the Post, *based it on screenplay by Harry Kleiner, which in turn was adapted from the original story by Otto Klements and J. L. Bixby. Movie won special effects Oscar.*

The year is 1995. Jan Benes, a brilliant scientist who holds the key to the survival of mankind, defects to the West with his secret. Despite every precaution, enemy agents launch a kamikaze attack on the defector. Although not killed, Benes lies near death, a blood clot in his brain. Conventional surgery is impossible; the clot must be destroyed by laser beams from *inside* the stricken man's brain. A submarine with five American medical specialists on board is miniaturized—atomically shrunk to the size of a single bacterium—and injected into Benes' bloodstream. They have just sixty minutes to complete the operation and leave the man's body before they begin to resume their normal size. The hazards are countless, and their chances of success are as infinitesimal as their tiny, intrepid vessel. They *must* not fail. But one of them is a traitor determined to sabotage the mission.   *(1966)*

Outside their miniature submarine Proteus, the medical team attempts to cut into the scientist's lung to escape suffocation. The movie was a basic "Perils of Pauline" melodrama given a science fiction setting.

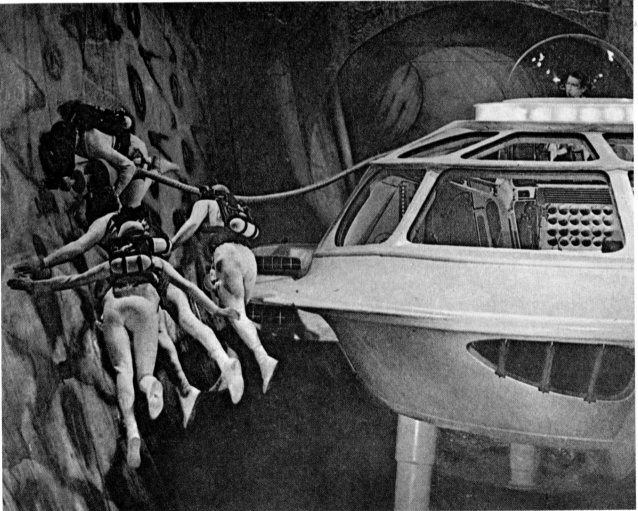

True Grit
by Charles Portis

When the officers were taking Wharton out he passed by Rooster Cogburn and said something to him, some ugly insult or threat, you could tell. Rooster just looked at him. The people pushed me on through the door and outside.

Rooster was one of the last ones out. He had a paper in one hand and a sack of tobacco in the other and he was trying to roll a cigarette. His hands were shaking and he was spilling tobacco.

I approached him and said, "Mr. Rooster Cogburn?"

He said, "What is it?" His mind was on something else.

I said, "They tell me you are a man with true grit."

He said, "What do you want, girl? Speak up. It is suppertime."

I said, "I am looking for the man who shot and killed my father, Frank Ross, in front of the Monarch boarding-house. The man's name is Tom Chaney. They say he is over in the Indian Territory and I need somebody to go after him."

He said, "What is your name, girl? Where do you live?"

"My name is Mattie Ross," I replied. "We are located in Yell County near Dardanelle. My mother is at home looking after my sister Victoria and my brother Little Frank."

"You had best go home to them," said he. "They will need some help with the churning."

I said, "The high sheriff and a man in the marshal's office have given me the full particulars. You can get a fugitive warrant for Tom Chaney and go after him. The government will pay you two dollars for bringing him in plus ten cents a mile for each of you. On top of that I will pay you a fifty-dollar reward."

"You have looked into this a right smart," said he.

"Yes, I have," said I. "I mean business."

He said, "What have you got there in your poke?"

I opened the sugar sack and showed him.

"By God!" said he. "A Colt's dragoon! Why, you are no bigger than a corn nubbin! What are you doing with that pistol?"

I said, "It belonged to my father. I intend to kill Tom Chaney with it if the law fails to do so. I am afraid nothing much is going to be done about him except I do it myself. Have you heard of a robber called Lucky Ned Pepper?"

"I know him well. I shot him in the lip last August down in the Winding Stair Mountains. He was plenty lucky that day."

"They think Tom Chaney has tied up with him."

"I don't believe you have fifty dollars, baby sister, but

if you are hungry I will give you supper and we will talk it over and make medicine. How does that suit you?"

I said it suited me right down to the ground. I figured he would live in a house with his family and was not prepared to discover that he had only a small room in the back of a Chinese grocery store on a dark street. He did not have a wife. The Chinaman was called Lee. He had a supper ready of boiled potatoes and stew meat. The three of us ate at a low table with a coal-oil lamp in the middle of it.

Rooster said he had heard about the shooting of my father but did not know the details. He ate with a spoon in one hand and a wadded-up piece of white bread in the other, with considerable sopping. What a contrast to the Chinaman with his delicate chopsticks! I had never seen them in use before. Such nimble fingers! When the coffee had boiled Lee got the pot off the stove and started to pour. I put my hand over my cup.

"I do not drink coffee, thank you."

Rooster said, "What do you drink?"

"I am partial to cold buttermilk when I can get it."

"Well, we don't have none," said he. "Nor lemonade either."

"Do you have any sweet milk?"

Lee went up front to his icebox and brought back a jar of milk. The cream had been skimmed from it.

I said, "This tastes like blue John."

I offered to clean things up and they took me at my word. The pump and the washstand were outside. When I got back inside, Rooster and Lee were playing cards on the table.

Rooster said, "Let me have my cup." I gave it to him and he poured some whiskey in it from a demijohn.

I said, "What about my proposition?"

Rooster said, "I am thinking on it."

I said, "It sounds like a mighty easy way to make fifty dollars to me. You would just be doing your job anyway, and getting extra pay besides."

"Don't crowd me," said he. "I am thinking about expenses."

He said, "If I am going up against Ned Pepper I will need a hundred dollars. I have figured out that much. I will want fifty dollars in advance."

"For that kind of money I would want to be sure of what I was getting."

"I have not yet seen the color of your money."

"I will have the money in a day or two. I will think

about your proposition and talk to you again. Now I want to go to the Monarch boardinghouse. You had better walk over there with me."

"If I had a big horse pistol like yours I would not be scared of any boogerman."

"I am not scared of the boogerman. I don't know the way over there."

"You are a lot of trouble. Wait till I finish this hand. You cannot tell what a Chinaman is thinking. That is how they beat you at cards."

They were betting money on the play and Rooster was not winning. I kept after him but he would only say, "One more hand," and pretty soon I was asleep with my head on the table. Some time later he began to shake me.

"Wake up," he was saying.

"What is it?" said I.

He was drunk and he was fooling around with Papa's pistol. He pointed out something on the floor over by the curtain that opened into the store. I looked and it was a big, long barn rat. He was eating meal that was spilling out of a hole in a sack. I gave a start but Rooster put his tobacco-smelling hand over my mouth and gripped my cheeks and held me down.

He said, "Be right still." I looked around for Lee and figured he must have gone to bed. Rooster said, "I will try this the new way. Now watch." He leaned forward and spoke at the rat in a low voice, saying, "I have a writ here that says for you to stop eating Chen Lee's cornmeal forthwith. It is a rat writ." Then he looked over at me and said, "Has he stopped?" I gave no reply. I have never wasted any time encouraging drunkards or show-offs. He said, "It don't look like to me he has stopped." He was holding Papa's revolver down at his side and he fired twice without aiming. The ear-splitting noise filled the room and made the curtains jump.

Lee sat up in his bunk and said, "Outside is place for shooting."

"I was serving some papers," said Rooster.

I said to Rooster, "Don't be shooting that pistol again. I don't have any more loads for it."

He said, "You would not know how to load it if you did have."

"I know how to load it."

He went to his bunk and pulled out a tin box that was underneath. He brought out some lead balls and little copper percussion caps and a tin of powder.

He said, "Let me see you do it."

"I don't want to right now. I am sleepy and I want to go to my quarters at the Monarch boardinghouse."

"Well, I didn't think you could," said he.

He said, "This piece is too big and clumsy for you."

He poked around in the bottom of the box and came up with a funny little pistol with several barrels. "Now this is what you need," he said. "It is a .22 pepperbox that shoots five times, and sometimes all at once. It is called 'The

"I don't believe you have fifty dollars," said Rooster (1969 movie starred John Wayne and Kim Darby).

Ladies' Companion.' There is a sporting lady called Big Faye in this city who was shot twice with it by her stepsister. Big Faye dressed out at about two hundred and ninety pounds. The bullets could not make it through to any vitals. That was unusual. It will give you good service against ordinary people. It is like new. I will trade you even for this old piece."

I said, "No, that was Papa's gun. I am ready to go. Do you hear me?" I took my pistol from him and put it back in the sack. He poured some more whiskey in his cup.

"You can't serve papers on a rat, baby sister."

"I never said you could."

"These shitepoke lawyers think you can but you can't. All you can do with a rat is kill him or let him be. They don't care nothing about papers. What is your thinking on it?"

"Are you going to drink all that?"

"Judge Parker knows. He is a old carpetbagger but he knows his rats. We had a good court here till pettifogging lawyers like Polk Goudy moved in on it. Now they have got the judge down on me. The rat-catcher is too hard on the rats. That is what they say. *Let up on them rats! Give them rats a fair show!* What kind of show did they give Columbus Potter? Tell me that." *(1968)*

Call of the Wild

by Jack London

As Buck slid along with the obscureness of a gliding shadow, his nose was jerked suddenly to the side as though a positive force had gripped and pulled it. He followed the new scent into a thicket and found Nig. He was lying on his side, dead where he had dragged himself, an arrow protruding, head and feathers, from either side of his body.

A hundred yards farther on, Buck came upon one of the sled-dogs John Thornton had bought in Dawson. This dog was thrashing about in a death-struggle, directly on the trail, and Buck passed around him without stopping. From the camp came the faint sound of many voices, rising and falling in a singsong chant. Bellying forward to the edge of the clearing, he found Hans, lying on his face, feathered with arrows like a porcupine. At the same instant Buck peered out where the spruce-bough lodge had been and saw what made his hair leap straight up on his neck and shoulders. A gust of overpowering rage swept over him. He did not know that he growled, but he growled aloud with a terrible ferocity. For the last time in his life he allowed passion to usurp cunning and reason, and it was because of his great love for John Thornton that he lost his head.

The Yeehats were dancing about the wreckage of the spruce-bough lodge when they heard a fearful roaring and saw rushing upon them an animal the like of which they had never seen before. It was Buck, a live hurricane of fury, hurling himself upon them in a frenzy to destroy. He sprang at the foremost man (it was the chief of the Yeehats), ripping the throat wide open till the rent jugular spouted a fountain of blood. He did not pause to worry the victim, but ripped in passing, with the next bound tearing wide the throat of a second man. There was no withstanding him. He plunged about in their very midst, tearing, rending, destroying, in constant and terrific motion which defied the arrows they discharged at him. In fact, so inconceivably rapid were his movements, and so closely were the Indians tangled together, that they shot one another with the arrows; and one young hunter, hurling a spear at Buck in mid air, drove it through the chest of another hunter with such force that the point broke through the skin of the back and stood out beyond. Then a panic seized the Yeehats, and they fled in terror to the woods, proclaiming as they fled the advent of the Evil Spirit.

And truly Buck was the Fiend incarnate, raging at their heels and dragging them down like deer as they raced through the trees. It was a fateful day for the Yeehats. They scattered far and wide over the country, and it was not till a week later that the last of the survivors gathered together in a lower valley and counted their losses. As for Buck, wearying of the pursuit, he returned to the desolated camp. He found Pete where he had been killed in his blankets in the first moment of surprise. Thornton's desperate struggle was fresh-written on the earth, and Buck scented every detail of it down to the edge of a deep pool. By the edge, head and fore feet in the water, lay Skeet, faithful to the last. The pool itself, muddy and discolored from the sluice boxes, effectually hid what it contained, and it contained John Thornton; for Buck followed his trace into the water, from which no trace led away.

All day Buck brooded by the pool or roamed restlessly above the camp. Death, as a cessation of movement, as a passing out and away from the lives of the living, he knew, and he knew John Thornton was dead. It left a great void in him, somewhat akin to hunger, but a void which ached and ached, and which food could not fill. At times, when he paused to contemplate the carcasses of the Yeehats, he forgot the pain of it; and at such times he was aware of a great pride in himself—a pride greater than any he had yet experienced. He had killed man, the noblest game of all, and he had killed in the face of the law of club and fang. He sniffed the bodies curiously. They had died so easily. It was harder to kill a husky dog than them. They were no match at all, were it not for their arrows and spears and clubs.

Night came on, and a full moon rose high over the trees into the sky, lighting the land till it lay bathed in ghostly day. And with the coming of the night, brooding and mourning by the pool, Buck became alive to a stirring of the new life in the forest other than that which the Yeehats had made. He stood up, listening and scenting. From far away drifted a faint, sharp yelp, followed by a chorus of similar sharp yelps. As the moments passed the yelps grew closer and louder. Again Buck knew them as things heard in that other world which persisted in his memory. It was the call, the many-noted call, sounding more luringly and compelling than ever before. And as never before, he was ready to obey. John Thornton was dead. The last tie was broken. Man and the claims of man no longer bound him.   *(1902)*

Jack Oakie and Clark Gable braved the deep freeze in Jack London's canine saga. Film also starred Loretta Young.

Lassie Come Home

by Eric Knight

For the first time in his trouble the boy became a child, and the mother, looking over, saw the tears that ran openly down his contorted face. She turned her face to the fire, and there was a pause. Then she spoke.

"Joe, tha mustn't," she said softly. "Tha must learn never to want nothing in life like that. It don't do, lad. Tha mustn't want things bad, like tha wants Lassie."

The boy shook his clenched fists in impatience.

"It ain't that, mother. Ye don't understand. Don't ye see—it ain't me that wants her. It's her that wants us! That's what made her come all them miles. It's her that wants us, so terrible bad!"

The woman turned and stared. It was as if, in that moment, she were seeing this child, this boy, this son of her own, for the first time in many years. She turned her head down toward the table. It was surrender.

"Come and eat, then," she said. "I'll talk to him. I will that, all right. I feel sure he won't lie. But I'll talk to him, all right. I'll talk to Mr. Joe Carraclough. I will indeed!"

At five that afternoon, the Duke of Rudling, fuming and muttering, got out of a car at a cottage gate to find a boy barring his way. This was a boy who stood, stubbornly, saying fiercely: "Away wi' thee! Thy tyke's net here!"

"Coom, coom, ma lad. Whet tyke's net here?"

"No tyke o' thine. Us hasn't got it." The words began running faster and faster as the boy backed away from the fearful old man who advanced. "No tyke could have done it. No tyke can come all them miles. It isn't Lassie. It's another one that looks like her. It isn't Lassie!"

"Why, bless ma heart and sawl," the duke puffed. "Where's thy father, ma lad?"

The door behind the boy opened, and a woman's voice spoke.

"If it's Joe Carraclough ye want, he's out in the shed—and been there shut up half the afternoon."

"What's this lad talking about—a dog of mine being here?"

"Nay," the woman snapped quickly. "He didn't say a tyke o' thine was here. He said it wasn't here."

"Well, what dog o' mine isn't here, then?"

With his mouth opening to cry one last protest, the boy turned. And his mouth stayed open. For there he saw his father, Joe Carraclough, the collie fancier, standing with a dog at his heels—a dog that sat at his left heel patiently, as any well-trained dog should—as Lassie used to do. But this dog was not Lassie. In fact, it was ridiculous to think of it at the same moment as you thought of Lassie.

For where Lassie's skull was aristocratic and slim, this dog's head was clumsy and rough. Where Lassie's ears stood in twin-lapped symmetry, this dog had one ear draggling and the other standing up Alsatian fashion in a way to give any collie breeder the cold shivers. Where Lassie's coat was rich tawny gold, this dog's coat had ugly patches of black; and where Lassie's apron was a billowing stretch of snow-white, this dog had puddles of off-color blue-merle mixture. Besides, Lassie had four white paws, and this one had one paw white, two dirty-brown, and one almost black.

That is the dog they all looked at as Joe Carraclough stood there, having told no lie, having only asked a question. They all stood, waiting the duke's verdict.

For a long time the duke stared, and when he got up he did not speak in Yorkshire accents anymore. He spoke as a gentleman should, and he said: "Joe Carraclough. I never owned this dog. 'Pon my soul, she's never belonged to me. Never!"

Then he turned and went stumping down the path, thumping his cane and saying: "Bless my soul. Four hundred miles! Damme, wouldn't ha' believed it."

He was at the gate when his granddaughter whispered to him fiercely.

"Of course," he cried. "Mind your own business. Exactly what I came for. Talking about dogs made me forget. Carraclough! Carraclough! What're ye hiding for?"

"I'm still here, sir."

"Ah, there you are. You working?"

"Eigh, now. Working," Joe said. That's the best he could manage.

"Yes, working, working!" The duke fumed.

"Well, now——" Joe began.

Then Mrs. Carraclough came to his rescue, as a good housewife in Yorkshire will.

"Why, Joe's got three or four things that he's been considering," she said, with proper display of pride. "But he hasn't quite said yes or no to any of them yet."

"Then say no, quick," the old man puffed. "Had to sack Hynes. Didn't know a dog from a drunken filly. Should ha' known all along no damn Londoner could handle dogs fit for Yorkshire taste. How much, Carraclough?"

"Seven pounds a week, and worth every penny," Mrs. Carraclough chipped in. "One o' them other offers may come up to eight," she lied, expertly. For there's always a certain amount of lying to be done in life, and when a woman's married to a man who has made a lifelong cult of being honest, then she's got to learn to do the lying for two.

"Five," roared the duke—who, after all, was a Yorkshireman, and couldn't help being a bit sharp about things that pertained to money.

"Six," said Mrs. Carraclough.

"Five pound ten," bargained the duke, cannily.

"Done," said Mrs. Carraclough, who would have been willing to settle for three pounds in the first place. "But o' course, us gets the cottage too."

The movie of Lassie *starred Roddy MacDowall and Elizabeth Taylor, and it germinated other films, television shows and a great vogue for collies.*

"All right," puffed the duke. "Five pounds ten and the cottage. Begin Monday. But—on one condition. Carraclough, you can live on my land, but I won't have that thick-skulled, screw-lugged, gay-tailed eyesore of a misshapen mongrel on my property. Now never let me see her again. You'll get rid of her?"

He waited, and Joe fumbled for words. But it was the boy who answered, happily, gaily: "Oh, no, sir. She'll be waiting at school for me most o' the time. And, anyway, in a day or so we'll have her fixed up and coped up so's ye'd never, never recognize her."

"I don't doubt that," puffed the duke, as he went to the car. "I don't doubt ye could do just exactly that, if ye had a mind to."

It was a long time afterward, in the car, that the girl said: "Don't sit there like a lion on the Nelson column. And I thought you were supposed to be a hard man."

"Fiddlesticks, m'dear. I'm a ruthless realist. For five years I've sworn I'd have that dog by hook or crook, and now, egad, at last I've got her."

"Pooh! You had to buy the man before you could get his dog."

"Well, perhaps that's not the worst part of the bargain."   *(1938)*

The Covered Wagon

by Emerson Hough

More than two thousand men, women and children waited on the Missouri for the green fully to tinge the grasses of the prairies farther west. The waning town of Independence had quadrupled its population in thirty days. Boats discharged their customary western cargo at the newer landing on the river, not far above that town; but it all was not enough. Men of Upper Missouri and Lower Iowa had driven in herds of oxen, horses, mules; but there were not enough of these. Rumors came that a

hundred wagons would take the Platte this year via the Council Bluffs, up the Missouri; others would join on from St. Jo and Leavenworth.

March had come, when the wild turkey gobbled and strutted resplendent in the forest lands. April had passed, and the wild fowl had gone north. May, and the upland plovers now were nesting all across the prairies. But daily had more wagons come, and neighbors had waited for neighbors, tardy at the great rendezvous. The encampment, scattered up and down the river front, had become more and more congested. Men began to know one another, families became acquainted, the gradual sifting and shifting in social values began. Knots and groups began to talk of some sort of accepted government for the common good.

They now were at the edge of the law. Organized society did not exist this side of the provisional government of Oregon, devised as a *modus vivendi* during the joint occupancy of that vast region with Great Britain—an arrangement terminated not longer than two years before. There must be some sort of law and leadership between the Missouri and the Columbia. Amid much bickering of petty politics Jesse Wingate had some four days ago been chosen for the thankless task of train captain. Though that office had small authority and less means of enforcing its commands, nonetheless the train leader must be a man of courage, resource and decision. Those of the earlier arrivals who passed by his well-organized camp of forty-odd wagons from the Sangamon country of Illinois said that Wingate seemed to know the business of the trail. His affairs ran smoothly, he was well equipped and seemed a man of means. Some said he had three thousand in gold at the bottom of his cargo. Moreover—and this appeared important among the Northern element, at that time predominant in the rendezvous—he was not a Calhoun Secesh, or even a Benton Democrat, but an out-and-out, antislavery, free-soil man. And the provisional constitution of Oregon, devised by thinking men of two great nations, had said that Oregon should be free soil forever.

All along the crooked river front, on both sides from

The first epic not directed by D. W. Griffith, **The Covered Wagon** *(1923), gave an enormous boost to Westerns.*

The **Post**'s great Western artist, W. H. D. Koerner, portrayed **Wagon**'s heroine, later played by Lois Wilson.

Independence to the river landing at Westport, the great spring caravan lay encamped, or housed in town. Now, on the last days of the rendezvous, a sort of hysteria seized the multitude. The sound of rifle fire was like that of a battle—every man was sighting-in his rifle. Singing and shouting went on everywhere. Someone fresh from the Mexican War had brought a drum, another a bugle. Without instructions these began to sound their summons and continued all day long, at such times as the performers could spare from drink.

The Indians of the friendly tribes—Otos, Kaws, Osages—come in to trade, looked on in wonder at the revelings of the whites. The straggling street of each of the nearby river towns was full of massed wagons. The treble line of white tops, end to end, lay like a vast serpent, curving, head to the West. Rivalry for the head of the column began. The sounds of the bugle set a thousand uncoordinated wheels spasmodically in motion. Organization, system were as yet unknown in this rude and dominant democracy. Need was therefore for this final meeting in the interest of law, order and authority. Already some wagons had broken camp and moved on.

To add yet more to the natural apprehensions of men and women embarking on so stupendous an adventure, all manner of rumors now continually passed from one company to another. It was said that five thousand Mormons, armed to the teeth, had crossed the river at St. Joseph and were lying in wait on the Platte, determined to take revenge for the persecutions they had suffered in Missouri and Illinois. Another story said that the Kaw Indians, hitherto friendly, had banded together for robbery and were only waiting for the train to appear. A still more popular story had it that a party of several Englishmen had hurried ahead on the trail to excite all the savages to waylay and destroy the caravans, thus to wreak the vengeance of England upon the Yankees for the loss of Oregon. Much unrest arose over reports, hard to trace, to the effect that it was all a mistake about Oregon; that in reality it was a truly horrible country, unfit for human occupancy, and sure to prove the grave of any lucky enough to survive the horrors of the trail, which never yet had been truthfully reported.

The Great Dipper showed clear and close that night, as if one might almost pick off by hand the familiar stars of the traveler's constellation. Overhead countless brilliant points of lesser light enameled the night mantle, matching the many camp fires of the great gathering. The wind blew soft and low. Night on the prairie is always solemn, and tonight the tense anxiety, the strained anticipation of more than two thousand souls invoked a brooding melancholy which it seemed even the stars must feel.

A dog, ominous, lifted his voice in a long, mournful howl which made mothers put out their hands to their babes. In answer a coyote raised a high, quavering cry, wild and desolate, the voice of the Far West.   *(1922)*

Commodore Hornblower

by C. S. Forester

There was a rapid exchange of dialogue between Clausewitz and the colonel, ending in the latter calling up two or three mounted officers—his adjutant and majors, perhaps—to accompany them up the road. Here they saw a larger infantry force formed up, and a line of guns, and here was a party on horseback, the feathers and braid and medals and mounted orderlies indicating the presence of a general's staff. This must be the General—Yorck, Hornblower remembered his name to be. He recognized Clausewitz at once, and addressed him abruptly in German. A few words on each side seemed only to add to the tension of the situation, and there was a short pause.

"He speaks French," said Clausewitz to Hornblower, and they both turned and waited for him to speak.

"General," said Hornblower; he was in a dream, but he made himself speak in his dream, "I represent the King of England, and Colonel Clausewitz represents the Emperor of Russia. We are fighting to free Europe from Bonaparte. Are you fighting to maintain him as a tyrant?"

It was a rhetorical question to which no answer was possible. Silent perforce, Yorck could only await the rest of what Hornblower had to say.

"Bonaparte is beaten. He is retreating from Moscow, and not ten thousand of his army will reach Germany. If you fight for him, you may keep him on his tottering throne for a few days longer. But your duty is to your enslaved country, to your King, who is a prisoner. You can free them. You can end the useless pouring out of the blood of your men now, at this moment."

Yorck looked away from him over the bleak countryside, at the Russian army slowly deploying, before he replied.

"What do you suggest?" he said.

That was all Hornblower desired. If Yorck was willing to ask questions, instead of immediately making prisoners of them, the matter was as good as settled. He brought Clausewitz into the conversation with a glance.

"An armistice," said Clausewitz. "An immediate suspension of hostilities."

Yorck still hesitated. Hornblower, despite his weariness and illness, could study him with a renewed flicker of interest; the hard face, sunburned to mahogany, the white hair and mustache in strange contrast. Yorck was on the edge of his fate. At present, he was a loyal subject of the King of Prussia, a comparatively undistinguished general. He had only to say two words, and they would make him a traitor now and conceivably a historic figure in the future. Prussia's defection would reveal the hollowness of the Napoleonic Empire.

"I agree," said Yorck.

That was all Hornblower wanted to hear. He could lapse into his dream—his nightmare—now, let the rest of the discussion take whatever course it would.

It was eight months since he had seen England; it seemed like a dream as he sat under his bearskin rug and saw the gray sands and then the low green hills of the Essex shore. It was market day in the town, and the streets were crowded as they walked slowly to The Crown. Hornblower sat over the fire in the coffeeroom with the conversation of garrulous farmers surging round him while Brown was hiring the post chaise.

The lodge keeper who opened the gates stood with gaping mouth at the sight of Hornblower, but his surprise was nothing compared with that of Wiggins when he threw open the door in answer to Brown's thundering upon it. He could not even say a word, but stood yammering before he drew aside to admit his master. There was the sound of singing in the hall, which was gay with holly and bright with candles. Apparently, his wife Barbara was entertaining the village carol singers.

"Glad ti-idings of com-fort and joy!" sang the carolers.

There was a rush of feet, and here was Barbara, and Barbara's arms were about his neck and Barbara's lips were upon his. And here came Richard, his steps hesitating a little, big-eyed and solemn and shy at the sight of this strange father of his.

Hornblower caught him up in his arms, and Richard continued to inspect him solemnly at close range.

"Glad tidings of comfort and joy," said Barbara, her hand on his arm.   *(1945)*

Gregory Peck was Hollywood's hero of sea adventures chronicled in the Post *between 1945 and 1957. Forester, who also wrote* The African Queen, *left an account of Hornblower's death to be published after his own.*

The Sea of Grass

by Conrad Richter

"We find," he drawled, "that Andy Boggs was shot at and run off the place he wanted to file on by unknown parties."

I saw the strict face of the judge redden over some impropriety.

"That's no verdict!" he reminded sharply. "The two defendants must——"

"Oh, hell, they're not guilty," Eli waved.

I wanted to give the Apache war whoop, while behind me a row of cow hands stamped their boots and jingled their spurs until Judge White pounded his pine bench in anger. Then he demanded the formal written verdict of the grinning jury foreman and adjourned court.

"Is that the verdict you wanted, Hal?" Lutie Cameron asked eagerly, but I saw that her eyes were not on me or our freed cow hands, rather on the tall young district attorney, who had winced as if thrown by a horse.

Another moment and she had urged me up from our bench. With her arm in mine, she swept up the aisle, chatting with animation at every step, and through the railing, where she stopped beside my uncle, slipping her free arm delicately through his, just as I saw Brice Chamberlain get himself in hand and stiffly congratulate Henry McCurtin.

Then the defeated young district attorney turned to my uncle.

"May I ask a few questions that I had no opportunity for during the trial, Colonel Brewton?"

His manner was courteous, but there was a faintly challenging ring in his voice and a blue fire in his eyes that kindled the silent attention of those of us standing inside of the railing. He went on without waiting for assent:

"Is it true, Colonel Brewton, that your range runs a hundred miles or more north and south, and west nearly to the Arizona line?"

My uncle merely inclined his head.

"Is it true," Chamberlain went on, his voice suddenly rising, "that of this vast country you control, you actually own only a few scattered water holes that have been filed on either in your name or those of your men? And that by far the great part still belongs to the Government?"

"Legally, yes," my uncle conceded.

"Is it true, then," Chamberlain concluded, his voice gathering force and indignation, "that this million or more of acres still belonging to the Government is the same land that Andrew Boggs, who only wanted a mere hundred and sixty acres for a homestead, was run off from and severely wounded by unknown parties?"

"No," my uncle said quietly, but with great firmness and power. "He was not run off because he wanted to settle those hundred and sixty acres, but because of what he wanted to do with the land."

Brice Chamberlain did not glance around. But something seemed to pass behind his brightly burning blue eyes. His manner changed. An appeal came into his face and voice, and standing there bent persuasively toward my uncle, even I, for a moment, thought him modest and almost likable.

"Let's forget about this case, Colonel Brewton. Andrew Boggs was only a single man and the court has disposed of him. Waiting at the edge of Salt Fork to see how this trial comes out are more than a dozen settlers. Not single men, but with families from babes at the breast to grandmothers. They have given up their homes in the East, driven their wagons more than a thousand miles across the plains and left their dead from the Mississippi to the Rio Grande—all with the one purpose of finding homes for themselves in this great territory." His voice grew eloquent with pleading. "Now that you have won your case, Colonel Brewton, and can afford to show your sympathy and charity, I want to ask, in the names of these families, if you won't let them settle undisturbed on a few acres out of the million or more of Government land on your range?"

I saw Lutie Cameron's eyes, soft under her veil, glance expectantly at my uncle. But he didn't see her. He had thrown up his head like an unruly lead steer smelling wolves or water.

"Chamberlain," he said, "I have sympathy for the pioneer settler who came out here and risked his life and family among the Indians. And I hope I have a little charity for the nester who waited until the country was safe and peaceable before he filed a homestead on someone else's range who fought for it. But"—and his voice began to ring in that small hushed courtroom, "when that nester picks country like my big *vega* that's more than seven thousand feet above the sea, when he wants to plow it up to support his family where there isn't enough rain for crops to grow, where he only kills the grass that will grow, where he starves for water and feeds his family by killing my beef, and becomes a man without respect to himself and a miserable menace to the territory, then I have neither sympathy nor charity!''

For nearly a minute more, the two men faced each other; one older, rugged and utterly fearless; the other, young and white with emotion.

"They warned me," Brice Chamberlain said, in a low burning voice, "not to bring action against you or your men. They told me there was no justice here, and you dominated the country and would never share your land with your less-fortunate fellow men."

He turned on his heel and left, but all of us knew that this was not the end. Then I looked at Lutie Cameron. She still hung on my uncle's arm, delicate, silent, rigid, her eyes on a stunned little group of listening Missourians in the patched blue and striped jumpers of farmers huddled there in the courtroom. And when she and my uncle went out to the hotel for dinner, I saw her take the spray of bright yellow blossoms she had pinned so gaily across her coat and throw it away.

With my hat hot and uncomfortable in my hand, I waited as long as I dared that afternoon outside the ladies' parlor of the Exchange House. When I pushed in the door,

Tracy, the red-headed Irishman, and Hepburn, the aristo-crat (here in The Sea of Grass) *first appeared together in 1941, became one of filmdom's great duos.*

I saw my uncle standing with dignity in front of the tall window. Beside him stood Lutie Cameron, her head thrown firmly up, her brown veil raised, her plumes at a high and gallant angle, making an unforgettable picture in that dark cavernous room with a single shaft of sunshine pouring over her, while Judge White, in a long black coat with broad silken lapels, kept sternly clearing his throat and compressing his lips as he read the unfamiliar marriage service.

Her cheeks were dusted as if with flour when she turned, but nothing else betrayed her as Doctor Reid, who, I think, must have denied himself liquor all afternoon for the occasion, bowed like the Virginian he was, over her hand, and wished her happiness. And Henry McCurtin, in fresh linen unsullied by a single tobacco stain, asked her jovially through his dun mustaches how she had managed to rope such a shy war horse.

She and my uncle took me to the depot, and the last thing I saw of Lutie Brewton, she was standing with one arm outstretched, waving her handkerchief gaily after me—a gesture I coldly declined to answer. But late that night, when the train was puffing through the dark New Mexican hills, I kept thinking about her in that walled island of ranch house on my lost sea of grass.   *(1936)*

The Devil and Daniel Webster

by Stephen Vincent Benét

Dan'l Webster looked in the jurors' eyes and knew it was him they'd come for, not only Jabez Stone. He stood there for a moment, his black eyes burning like anthracite. And then he began to speak.

He started off in a low voice, though you could hear every word. They say he could call on the harps of the blessed when he chose. And this was just as simple and easy as a man could talk. But he didn't start out by condemning or reviling. He was talking about the things

that make a country a country, and a man a man.

And he began with the simple things that everybody's known and felt—the freshness of a fine morning when you're young, and the taste of food when you're hungry, and the new day that's every day when you're a child. He took them up and he turned them in his hands. They were

Edward Arnold was Daniel Webster, Walter Huston was the devil in the movie, **All That Money Can Buy** *(1941). Also starred: James Craig, Simone Simon.*

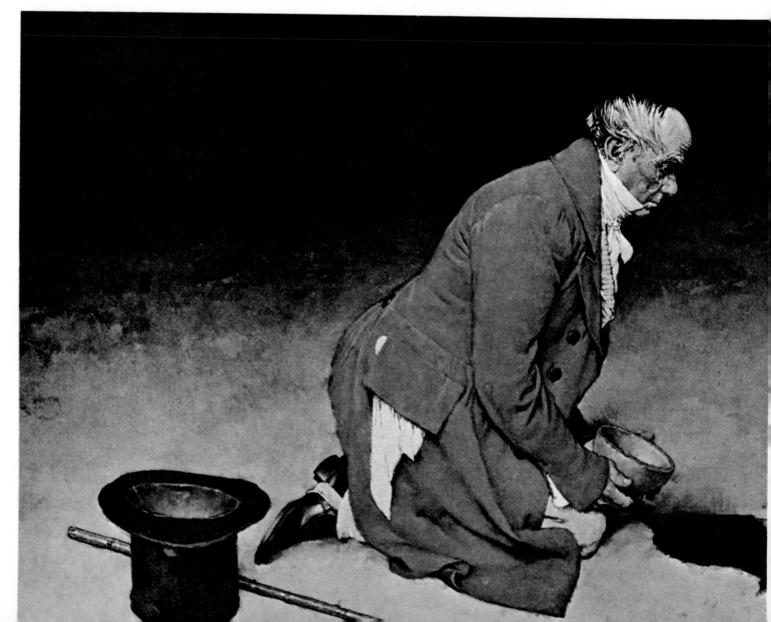

good things for any man. But without freedom, they sickened. And when he talked of those enslaved, and the sorrows of slavery, his voice got like a big bell. He talked of the early days of America and the men who had made those days. It wasn't a spread-eagle speech, but he made you see it. He admitted all the wrong that had ever been done. But he showed how, out of the wrong and the right, the suffering and the starvations, something new had come. And everybody had played a part in it, even the traitors.

Then he turned to Jabez Stone and showed him as he was—an ordinary man who'd had hard luck and wanted to change it. And, because he'd wanted to change it, now he was going to be punished for eternity. And yet there was good in Jabez Stone, and he showed that good. He was hard and mean, in some ways, but he was a man. There was sadness in being a man, but it was a proud thing too. And he showed what the pride of it was till you couldn't help feeling it. Yes, even in hell, if a man was a man, you'd know it. And he wasn't pleading for any one person anymore, though his voice rang like an organ. He was telling the story and the failures and the endless journey of mankind. They got tricked and trapped and bamboozled, but it was a great journey. And no demon that was ever

foaled could know the inwardness of it—it took a man to do that.

The fire began to die on the hearth and the wind before morning to blow. The light was getting gray in the room when Dan'l Webster finished. And his words came back at the end to New Hampshire ground, and the one spot of land that each man loves and clings to. He painted a picture of that, and to each one of that jury he spoke of things long forgotten. For his voice could search the heart, and that was his gift and his strength. And to one, his voice was like the forest and its secrecy, and to another like the sea and the storms of the sea; and one heard the cry of his lost nation in it, and another saw a little harmless scene he hadn't remembered for years. But each saw something. And when Dan'l Webster finished he didn't know whether or not he'd saved Jabez Stone. But he knew he'd done a miracle. For the glitter was gone from the eyes of judge and jury, and, for the moment, they were men again, and knew they were men.

"The defense rests," said Dan'l Webster, and stood there like a mountain. His ears were still ringing with his speech, and he didn't hear anything else till he heard Judge Hathorne say, "The jury will retire to consider its verdict."

Walter Butler rose in his place and his face had a dark,

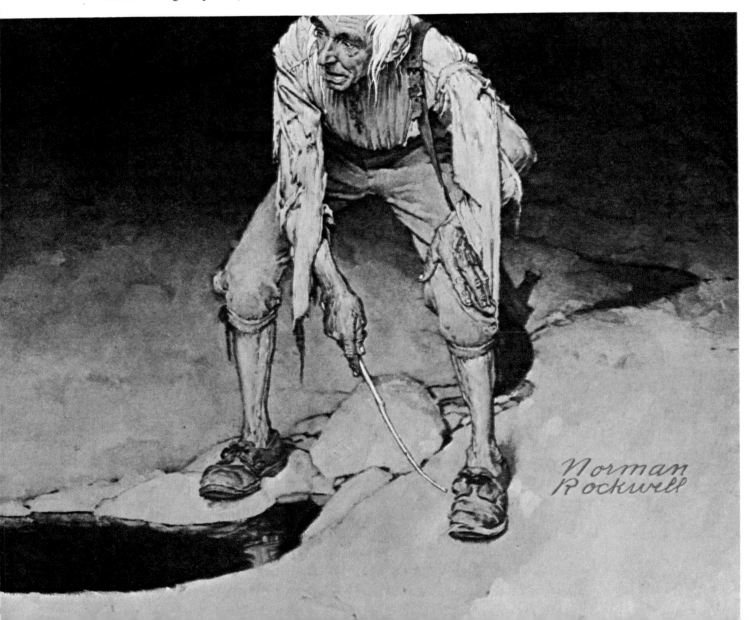

gay pride on it as he spoke to the assembly.

"The jury has considered its verdict," he said, and looked the stranger full in the eye. "We find for the defendant, Jabez Stone."

With that, the smile left the stranger's face, but Walter Butler did not flinch.

"Perhaps 'tis not strictly in accordance with the evidence," he said, "but even the damned may salute the eloquence of Mr. Webster."

With that, the long crow of a rooster split the gray morning sky, and judge and jury were gone from the room like a puff of smoke and as if they had never been there. The stranger turned to Dan'l Webster, smiling wryly.

"Major Butler was always a bold man," he said. "I had not thought him quite so bold. Nevertheless, my congratulations, as between two gentlemen."

"I'll have that paper first, if you please," said Dan'l Webster, and he took it and tore it into four pieces. It was queerly warm to the touch. "And now," he said, "I'll have you!" and his hand came down like a bear trap on the stranger's arm. For he knew that once you bested anybody like Mr. Scratch in fair fight, his power on you was gone. And he could see that Mr. Scratch knew it too.

The stranger twisted and wriggled, but he couldn't get out of that grip. "Come, come, Mr. Webster," he said, smiling palely. "This sort of thing is ridic—ouch!—is ridiculous. If you're worried about the costs of the case, naturally, I'd be glad to pay——"

"And so you shall!" said Dan'l Webster, shaking him till his teeth rattled. "For you'll sit right down at that table and draw up a document, promising never to bother Jabez Stone nor his heirs or assigns nor any other New Hampshireman till doomsday! For any hades we want to raise in this state, we can raise ourselves, without assistance from strangers."

"Ouch!" said the stranger. "Ouch! Well, they never did run very big to the barrel, but—ouch!—I agree!"

So he sat down and drew up the document. But Dan'l Webster kept his hand on his coat collar all the time.

"And, now, may I go?" said the stranger, quite humble, when Dan'l'd seen the document's in proper and legal form.

"Go?" said Dan'l, giving him another shake. "I'm still trying to figure out what I'll do with you. For you've settled the costs of the case, but you haven't settled with me. I think I'll take you back to Marshfield," he said, kind of reflective. "I've got a ram there named Goliath that can butt through an iron door. I'd kind of like to turn you loose in his field and see what he'd do."

Well, with that the stranger began to beg and to plead. And he begged and he pled so humbly that finally Dan'l, who was naturally kindhearted, agreed to let him go. The stranger seemed terrible grateful for that and said, just to show they were friends, he'd tell Dan'l's fortune before leaving. So Dan'l agreed to that, though he didn't take much stock in fortune-tellers ordinarily. But, naturally, the stranger was a little different.

Well, he pried and he peered at the lines in Dan'l's hands. And he told him one thing and another that was quite remarkable. But they were all in the past.

"Yes, all that's true, and it happened," said Dan'l Webster. "But what's to come in the future?"

The stranger grinned, kind of happily, and shook his head.

"The future's not as you think it," he said. "It's dark. You have a great ambition, Mr. Webster."

"I have," said Dan'l firmly, for everybody knew he wanted to be President.

"It seems almost within your grasp," said the stranger, "but you will not attain it. Lesser men will be made President and you will be passed over."

"And, if I am, I'll still be Daniel Webster," said Dan'l. "Say on."

"You have two strong sons," said the stranger, shaking his head. "You look to found a line. But each will die in war and neither reach greatness."

"Live or die, they are still my sons," said Dan'l Webster. "Say on."

"You have made great speeches," said the stranger. "You will make more."

"Ah," said Dan'l Webster.

"But the last great speech you make will turn many of your own against you," said the stranger. "They will call you Ichabod; they will call you by other names. Even in New England, some will say you have turned your coat and sold your country, and their voices will be loud against you till you die."

"So it is an honest speech, it does not matter what men say," said Dan'l Webster. Then he looked at the stranger and their glances locked.

"One question," he said. "I have fought for the Union all my life. Will I see that fight won against those who would tear it apart?"

"Not while you live," said the stranger, grimly, "but it will be won. And after you are dead, there are thousands who will fight for your cause, because of words that you spoke."

"Why, then, you long-barreled, slab-sided, lantern-jawed, fortune-telling note shaver!" said Dan'l Webster, with a great roar of laughter, "be off with you to your own place before I put my mark on you! For, by the thirteen original colonies, I'd go to the Pit itself to save the Union!"

And with that he drew back his foot for a kick that would have stunned a horse. It was only the tip of his shoe that caught the stranger, but he went flying out of the door with his collecting box under his arm.

"And now," said Dan'l Webster, seeing Jabez Stone beginning to rouse from his swoon, "let's see what's left in the jug, for it's dry work talking all night. I hope there's pie for breakfast, Neighbor Stone."

But they say that whenever the devil comes near Marshfield, even now, he gives it a wide berth. And he hasn't been seen in New Hampshire from that day to this. I'm not talking about Massachusetts or Vermont.   *(1936)*

Tugboat Annie
by Norman Reilly Raine

"I'm fired? Who says I'm fired?" Tugboat Annie Brennan leaned across the desk of the president of the Deep-Sea Towing and Salvage Company, and thrust her formidable jowls into his red, embarrassed face. She repeated, with husky emphasis: "Who says so?"

"Now, Annie! Please——"

"Don't you 'Now, Annie' me, Alec Severn! And answer my question!"

Mr. Severn coughed, and mopped his perspiring brow "Well—hrrmph! It's Mr. Conroy. The business needs money, and he's putting it in—a lot of it. Enough to buy that new tugboat we want so badly. He's an absolute godsend. But he's got ideas—about women, I mean."

"Huh! What man hasn't? And what is these fool ideas?"

"Well, he—he thinks that managing a towing and salvage company is a man's job. He has the notion that women lack the—well, intelligence was the word he used—to handle the active side of the business. Says men won't do their maximum of efficient work under a woman chief. They resent her."

Tugboat Annie snorted, "I'd like to see any o' the boys on the *Narcissus* resent me. I'd heave 'em——"

"I know—I know! But Mr. Conroy doesn't understand. You and I belong to the old school, Annie, and our ways don't seem to fit these days somehow. Mr. Conroy, now, he's modern. He is efficient and understands modern business methods." He hesitated and lowered his voice: "Tell you the truth, Annie, I don't fancy the man. There's something about him—cold. If there was any other way of getting the money I'd see him in—I mean, I wouldn't have him! But there isn't. And he thinks that—Wait a minute. Here he comes up the stairs. He can tell you himself—thank the Lord." He concluded.

Tugboat Annie drew herself up and glared, first out the window, to the crowded shipping of the harbor and the busy wharves, and then at the office door. She was large-framed, solidly built, with rugged, almost masculine features, and shrewd, quick, blue eyes, and her movements had an elephantine energy that galvanized everyone with whom she came in contact. When she passed through a room, dust and odd bits of paper danced in her wake. And when she stood, she looked not unlike a blowzy but exceedingly combative bulldog.

Marie Dressler as Tugboat Annie was the movies' biggest attraction in 1932 and '33, beating out Garbo, with whom she had starred in Eugene O'Neill's Anna Christie.

The door opened and Severn held his breath. Mr. Conroy entered, a businessman from his crisp, graying hair, precisely parted, to his efficiently polished English oxfords. Mr. Conroy liked to convey the impression of a micrometrically functioning, hard-glazed piece of steel mechanism; and his impersonation was highly successful.

"Morning, Severn," he said crisply; but Tugboat Annie heaved herself forward.

"Say!" she demanded. "Are you the lallapaloosa that says I'm fired?"

Mr. Conroy drew back, hastily adjusting his glasses. "Why, I'm afraid I don't understand."

"Neither do I. Neither does Alec. So who does?"

Severn said, placatingly, "This is Mrs. Brennan, Mr. Conroy. You remember we discussed her——"

"Tugboat Annie Brennan! That's what the waterfront calls me. And I didn't get the name pushin' toy boats around the bathtub, either! Now, what you firin' me for?"

Severn interposed again: "You see, Conroy, Mrs. Brennan's husband, Terry, was senior captain of the company for a good many years. He was a good tugboat man, but——"

"Terry was a drunken sot. But he was the best husband a woman ever had, Lord rest his soul! And in between his rasslin' bouts with old John——"

"John?" said Conroy, with raised eyebrows.

"Barleycorn!" said Tugboat Annie briefly. "In between bouts I ran his job for him. A year ago he died o'——"

"Syncope," Severn hastily interpolated.

"Water poisonin'!" Tugboat Annie corrected grimly. "Drank a glass o' water, thinkin' it was gin, and his stomach couldn't stand the shock. Alec let me stay in his place, and I done a good job of it, too. Ain't I, Alec?"

During the recital Conroy's thin lips had tightened to an obdurate line.

"The opinion I expressed to you yesterday, Severn, has not altered. It has been strengthened. To be quite frank, Mrs.—er—Brennan does not impress me. She is too—shall we say, informal? I propose, if I enter this company, to make it the strongest on the seaboard, and the position of senior captain will be one of responsibility, dignity. No doubt she knows something about the work. But she is a woman, and—in this business particularly—that is not a good thing."

Tugboat Annie choked.

Wallace Beery and his typical "Aw, shucks" reply won an Oscar (for The Champ*) and teamed up with Marie Dressler twice, in* Tugboat Annie *and in* Min and Bill*.*

"Her influence, in what essentially is a man's sphere, is bound to have undesirable results. I think I can see it, even now, in small things. The names of your present vessels, for instance. Tugs connote strength; rude but efficient power. And instead of calling them appropriate names, such as, say, *Trojan, Titan, Atlas, Hercules,* they are called"—he smiled acridly—"*Daffodil, Asphodel, Pansy* and *Narcissus.*"

"What of it? Can't a person like posies?"

"May I remind you that I am not deaf?"

"Mebbe you're not, but you're awful dumb! Here I've give twenty years of my life to the company and you come along and I'm throwed out like an old sweat rag. Didn't it ever occur to you, Mr. Conman, or whatever your name is, that loyalty and hard work's worth something to business, as well as a lot o' fancy names? Huh? . . . Oh, well! What's the good o' spinnin' me jaw? When do I go, Alec?"

"Go back to the *Narcissus,* Annie," said Severn unhappily "I'll let you know. I'm sorry—"

Conroy moved apprehensively aside as Tugboat Annie barged toward him, but she passed without a word and went down the stairs.

Crossing the railroad tracks, she got one shoe half full of gravel, which did not improve her temper. She limped painfully out on the long, dingy wharf and stopped to remove the gravel from her shoe. She shook the shoe irascibly, and it flew from her grasp and disappeared with a splash into the dock. Tugboat Annie watched it sink, her lips moving wordlessly, then limped on her stockinged foot, great toe protruding, the length of the wharf. *(1931)*

Movie Masters

Colossus of Celluloid

by John Durant

"The show was over at seven and we stepped into the weirdest city I had ever seen. London looked like a technicolor production of *The Burning of Rome* by Cecil B. De Mille. It was so garish as to be a little bit overdramatized and in bad taste."

An American newspaperman cabled those words from England while London was still in flaming ruins. It was the Great Fire of 1940 and when the newspaperman, William L. White, of the *Emporia Gazette*, walked out of a theater

into the middle of it, he could not at first find a word to fit the frightful magnitude of the scene. Then he thought of De Mille. It was the exact word, not only one which meant the flamboyant, the spectacular and the unreal, but one which was familiar to millions of people the world over. If De Mille has accomplished nothing else, he has at least enriched the English language, for his name is commonly used to describe such things as the Grand Canyon, the Mississippi flood, an onyx bathroom or a Palm Beach debutante party.

In his time he's seen great directors come to the fore and fade into obscurity—David Wark Griffith, James Cruze, George Fitzmaurice and others. The old man has outlasted them all, and today, at the zenith of his career, he's spending more money, getting more back in the till and is more super-super in his productions than ever before.

Despite his power at the box office, De Mille has never won a Motion Picture Academy Award. Nor have any of the writers, stars, actors or actresses in supporting roles in any of his pictures ever gone home from the Academy dinner with an Oscar.

"I win my Oscars at the box office," De Mille says.

The New York Film Critics, an association which annually selects the year's best picture, has persistently ignored De Mille. His answer to that body and to critics in general is: "Every time I make a picture, the critics' estimation of the public drops another ten degrees."

Yet De Mille is not wholly without honors for his achievements. He has his footprints planted in the forecourt of Grauman's Chinese Theater side by side with Al Jolson's knee and Rin Tin Tin's paws.

It is over the weekends, when De Mille retires to his ranch, that he discards the conservative garb of the family man and assumes a more theatrical role to become the master of Paradise. De Mille has never admitted newspapermen to his ranch. There is no telephone on the place and cameras are taboo. Many exaggerated stories have arisen about the strange customs and rituals that take place there.

When directors' names were unknown, De Mille's was a household word. Specializing in epics, he made 70 movies.

Upon arrival each male guest was outfitted with a satin Russian blouse of vivid hue, to be worn with the trousers of his own dinner suit. The ladies wore dinner gowns. De Mille himself often appeared in a voluminous black cape with two great gold buttons at the throat, and beneath it a crimson blouse. When the cape was thrown off, a revolver and cartridge belt were revealed—there are rattlesnakes between the main house and his sleeping lodge.

In the large room where the guests assembled, a great spruce fire crackled on the hearth, and fat cathedral candles burned beneath the rafters. Music drifted softly from a push-button Aztec organ. But De Mille apparently felt that the setting was enough to amuse his guests. Shortly after dinner he usually threw on his black cape and retired to the privacy of his stone lodge.

It is his boast he would not ask an actor to do anything in his pictures he himself would refuse to do.

In making *The Plainsman*, Jean Arthur, as Calamity Jane, had to wield a twelve-foot bull whip and flick a revolver out of a bad man's hand. De Mille saw that the gunman did not relish exposing his arm, and possibly his face, to Miss Arthur's inexperienced lashes. De Mille of-

De Mille (with Chaplin and the Mountbattens) was the first director to use megaphone, loudspeaker on the set.

fered his own arm and stood immobile while the star took several vigorous cuts at him with the rawhide. He suffered a bleeding forearm, but Miss Arthur was able to go through with the scene perfectly the first time it was shot.

At the Academy dinner at which the guest of honor was Dr. Hu Shih, the Chinese ambassador, De Mille, in the middle of his speech, turned toward the Chinese scholar and, looking him right in the eye, said, "It is our rare privilege to have the Japanese ambassador with us this evening."

The concerted gasps from the cinema great sounded like a waterfall in the spring. De Mille stopped and, crimson-faced, said, "I meant, of course, the Chinese ambassador."

The next day telephones hummed, Hollywood columnists gave the incident top billing and many bigwigs of the industry demanded that De Mille write a note of apology to the ambassador.

De Mille felt dreadfully alone that evening as he sat in his study at home, suffering beyond proportion to the incident. The door opened and a lady quietly entered. It was his Gretchen. Placing her hand on his shoulder, she smiled, "Well, anyway, Cecil, at last you've done something Hollywood will always remember you by." *(1943)*

Louie B.
by William Saroyan

A man named Louis B. Mayer once ran a movie studio named Metro-Goldwyn-Mayer. The Goldwyn was for Sam, who had long since gone into movie production on his own; the Mayer was for L. B. himself, and the Metro I have never been able to figure out.

Old L. B. gypped me, but as he *had* to, as he had no choice in the matter, as it would have killed him had he so much as *tried* not to gyp me, I don't see how I can hold it against him, or fail to notice that in his own way he was a big man. He wasn't a great man, but he was a big one. When he died, a Hollywood wit noticed the crowd at his funeral and said, "Give the public what they want and they'll be there every time." This was a paraphrase of a remark of the

deceased himself on how to make a successful movie.

Well, the fact is his movies *were* successful, and perhaps it doesn't matter that they were bad, too. He is the subject of at least one biography in which he is openly hated, even though the writer does not appear to have known him or to have been gypped by him. Apparently L. B. became a symbol of something that needed to be hated—a symbol, perhaps, of the contemptible power of money to maim, kill and corrupt. If that's so, then there are few people in America worth $50,000 or more who are not eligible for this same hatred. And I doubt if many of them could compare with L. B. in the possession of a variety of redeeming qualities.

For one thing, he could act.

He could out-act any actor at his studio, as he once bragged to me after a meeting in his office with one of his unhappy stars. Among others, his stars were Clark Gable, Spencer Tracy, Robert Taylor, Lionel Barrymore, Wallace Beery, Frank Morgan, Mickey Rooney; and a dozen or more actresses, including Greta Garbo, Joan Crawford, Norma Shearer, Jean Harlow and Carole Lombard.

He had *made* that studio. It was his. He had made that movie factory, that dream factory, that lie factory, and if you couldn't care for the product, you also couldn't deny that millions of others *did* care for it. And you couldn't deny that the product had earned millions of dollars for the big fat corporations, and made dozens of fantastic reputations.

"Make this world heaven," he wept, "and I'll be the first angel in the land. I'll spend all my time on my knees, like this, thanking God for making a world so right and true. I won't be a gangster among a lot of pickpockets and pimps; I'll be the best angel God ever saw, but don't expect *me* to make heaven out of this world. I can't do it. It's not my line. I make movies. I make the best and biggest money-making movies in the world."

He *had* to gyp me, that is, because he had long since gypped himself in agreeing with himself or with his own belittlers and rivals in the business jungle that nothing, nothing, absolutely nothing is worth more than money and the things it can buy dirt cheap, especially people, especially himself, a big animal in the biggest cage in the biggest zoo in the world, living well and dying of loneliness, meaninglessness and despair.   *(1963)*

He listened to Mrs. Mayer, at least. At Hollywood's biggest studio his word was law from 1924 to 1951.

Mr. Malaprop
by Alva Johnston

Some of the true Goldwyn lines are a credit to him. He can often put things more forcefully in his own medium of expression than they could possibly be said in the king's English. An ordinary man, on deciding to quit the Hays organization, might have turned to his fellow producers and said, "Gentlemen, I prefer to stand aloof," or "Gentlemen, I have decided to go my own way." Sam said, "Gentlemen, include me out." It would be impossible to make a more pointed remark than Goldwyn's "A verbal contract isn't worth the paper it's written on." One day, after slicing five or six golf balls, he made a beautiful drive; he turned to the caddie and asked, "What did I do right?"

Most of Sam's word trouble is inattention. His mind is usually 90 or 100 percent occupied with future pictures. In the very act of telling Louis Bromfield how important the name of Bromfield was, Sam called him Bloomfield. When hiring Arthur Hornblow, Jr., Sam called him Hornbloom. Hornblow wrote the name on a paper; Sam waved it aside, saying, "Show me later." Ben Cahane, a member of the Goldwyn organization, was always "Mr. Cocoon." When Charlie Chaplin returned from Paris several years ago, Sam inquired after the health of Anatole France by asking, "How are the Affairs of Anatole?" Shirley Temple is Anne Shirley to Goldwyn; King Vidor is Henry King.

On one trip he found distinguished foreigners lionizing him to a degree that worried him. "Over there," he said, "they kept watching my mouth all the time, expecting something funny to pop out."

They were disappointed. Sam goes sometimes for days without saying anything memorable. He usually has to be pretty excited in order to coin anything that will live. He does have good days, however. Here are a few Goldwyn lines that are vouched for by good authorities:

"The trouble with this business is the dearth of bad pictures."

"We can get all the Indians we need at the reservoir."

"Our new executive was born in an orpheum asylum."

"My horse was in the lead, coming down the homestretch, when the caddie had to fall off."

"Excuse me, I am going out for some tea and trumpets."

"That's the way with these directors; they're always biting the hand that lays the golden egg."

"You're always taking the bull between the teeth."

Samuel Goldwyn shared the golden touch. Among his hits: **Wuthering Heights, The Best Years of Our Lives.**

"I have been laid up with intentional flu."

"He treats me like the dirt under my feet."

"I would be sticking my head in a moose."

"I want to make a picture about the Russian Secret Police—the G. O. P."

"I had a monumental idea this morning, but I didn't like it."

He embarrassed a lady writer once by saying "cohabit" when he meant "cooperate."

"It's too caustic," said a director, when asked his opinion of a script.

"To hell with the cost," replied Sam. "If it's a good picture, we'll make it."　　　　　*(1937)*

From: David O.
by Alva Johnston

David O. Selznick rose to the top in Hollywood by one of the most exasperating habits a man can have. He is a memorandum addict. The habit has grown on him to such an extent that, in producing *Gone With the Wind,* he dictated more than 1,500,000 words of memos.

He fulminates at two stenographers. The first takes notes until her arm is tired, then the second works until the first has recovered, and so on. Selznick is probably the greatest living orator for output. His only competitors are one or two pulp-fiction authors.

His memos vary from paragraphs to book length. Clark Gable was routed out of bed at three o'clock one morning by a motorcycle messenger who presented him with what

looked like a typewritten history of the world. It proved to be a memo concerning the part of Rhett Butler to be read by Gable before appearing at the studio later that morning. Gable and others finally revolted and established a nine p.m. curfew on Selznick manifestoes.

Selznick was a child magnate when he contracted the memo habit. He used to work after school at the studio of his father, Lewis J. Selznick, a movie king of the silent days. In personal conferences with men two or three times his age, he suffered from self-consciousness. His typewriter became a sort of ambush. Hiding his immaturity behind the typewriter, he rattled off his ideas in showers of memos.

When he began to learn showmanship under his father's guidance, David became convinced that the sound and typographical appearance of a name were important. He became dissatisfied with his own designation, which was plain David Selznick, and felt that a middle initial would help. He experimented scientifically, testing the sound of every letter in the alphabet, like a songwriter trying out musical notes. *O* was the best. It had a strong, broad sound; it was necessary to pause in pronouncing it, and it gave a more impressive rhythm to the name. As soon as he felt sure that this would stick in the public memory better than any other of the twenty-six letters, he became David O. Selznick. This has registered so well that some of his mail comes addressed to David O'Selznick.

Selznick broke into cinema history in 1935 when he made *David Copperfield.* This was an important landmark, because it was the first convincing demonstration that a great classic can be made over into a successful film without throwing most of the original out the window.

In one of his memos reproaching writers for tampering with a great contemporary novel, Selznick set forth his philosophy as follows:

"The millions of people who have read the book and who worship it would very properly attack us violently for the desecrations which are indicated by this treatment; but quite apart from the feelings of these few million, I have never been able to understand why motion-picture people insist upon throwing away something of proven appeal to substitute things of their own creation. It is a form of ego which has drawn upon Hollywood the wrath of the world for many years."   *(1942)*

Selznick's special genius was for casting—the actors in his films seemed born for the roles they played.

Capra Can

by Alva Johnston

Capra was in San Francisco, playing poker for a living, when he read a news article about the plans of the newly organized Montague Film Company. He had at that time one of the blankest minds in America on the subject of movies. Though reared in Hollywood, he had visited a studio only once. Frank dropped in, however, at the Montague studio.

"I'm interested in what you're doing here," he said. "I happen to be from Hollywood."

Capra carried himself with the modest air of importance which a seller of wildcat stock tries to cultivate. Producer Montague, an old Shakespearean actor, was grateful for a chance to explain his plan to a man from Hollywood. He had for a long time cherished the belief that the public would like short motion pictures based on well-known poems.

"What do you think of the idea?" asked Montague.

"It's all right," said Capra.

Frank found himself in agreement with everything Montague said until the producer told how he planned to shoot the picture. He planned to rehearse his actors thoroughly and shoot the fifteen minutes of action without stopping.

"A motion-picture camera only runs four minutes," Capra said. "Then you have to stop and put in a new film."

The head of the Montague Film Company was staggered by this information. It was the only fact about the movies that Capra knew, but it established him as a mine of technical information. Before the conversation was over, Capra had been engaged for seventy-five dollars a week as technical adviser.

Capra later became one of the prisoners in the famous tower where Mack Sennett incarcerated his writers. Sennett used to prowl up four flights of steps and burst in on them to discover who was asleep. This went on until the gag writers used their gag technique for their own protection. They had a carpenter make one step higher than the others. Sennett always stumbled over it and rose cursing, giving each literary dormouse a chance to wake up a-scribbling. The Sennett organization was the greatest school for writers and stars that Hollywood ever had. Capra made rapid progress.

Capra's vagabondage, his homebred musical knowl-

edge, his Hans Christian Andersen quality of storytelling all came to his assistance in making *It Happened One Night*. One of the finest scenes was the bus ride. Outside, it was raining torrents; inside, cozy and sociable. When Capra likes a scene, he lets himself go. He played over endless phonograph records in search of hearty old tunes, and in this way unearthed "The Daring Young Man on the Flying Trapeze," an ancient piece that became a new sensation. Long drawn out as the bus scene was, it paid its way dramatically; the characters kept developing as the bus lurched on, until the driver, joining in the chorus, forgot to watch the road and had a smashup, which started the picture off on a new sequence. *(1938)*

A director who could write superb dialogue and skillfully edit film, Capra (left, with Hitchcock) used his talents on hits like Mr. Deeds Goes to Town, Lost Horizon.

Hitch-shock

by Pete Martin

The small round man who occupied the office had a long pink nose and a slow voice that wheezed as he talked. He was neither Capra nor Wyler. Instead, he was his own highly individual self, but a number of intelligent people believe that in his own bailiwick Alfred Hitchcock has no remote rival as a directorial genius.

I'd been trying to see him for a week, but he'd been very ill. Then he was reported convalescent. At last I got the word if I'd be at Paramount at three o'clock the following afternoon, he'd be happy to talk to me. When I saw him he looked amazingly well. I was surprised. I'd met him once before while covering the Hollywood beat and he looked better now than he had then.

"I hear you had more than one operation," I said. "Coming one on top of the other, they must have been quite a shock."

"The biggest shock was the indignities to which institutions of healing subject your person," he told me. "I'm not a squeamish man, but some of the things they do to you in hospitals are no less than obscene. When they came in to prepare me for surgery and tied a label on my wrist with my name on it, I thought, *They must think I'm ready for the morgue.*

" 'It isn't that,' they told me, laughingly. 'We just don't want you to get mixed up with anyone else and have the wrong operation.' That in itself was a thought-provoking notion.

"I had colitis, which was painful, and I'd had an umbilical hernia for years, and I had done nothing about either. I had those things taken care of; then I developed a pain in another place and I had jaundice. So, after profound study, the medical brains decided, 'You must have stones in your gall bladder,' and they took those out too. Their attitude reminded me strongly of the fight manager who says to his pug, 'Get in that ring and slug it out, boy. They can't hurt us.' "

"Speaking of physical indignities," I said, "it seems to me that the way various people describe you comes under that heading. Your nose has been called pendulous, your lower lip has been compared with a sugar scoop. If I asked you to describe yourself physically, how would you do it?"

"A New York doctor once told me that I'm an adrenal type," he said. "That apparently means that I'm all body and only vestigial legs. But since I'm neither a mile runner nor a dancer and my present interest in my body is almost altogether from the waist up, that didn't bother me.

"In selecting the stories for my television shows, I try to make them as meaty as the sponsor and the network will stand for. I hope to offset any tendency toward the macabre with humor. As I see it, that is a typically English form of humor; even a typically London type of humor. It's of a piece with such jokes as the one about the man who was being led to the gallows to be hanged. He looked at the trap door in the gallows, which was flimsily constructed, and he asked in some alarm, 'I say, is that thing safe?'

"A story about the comedian, Charles Coborn, is cut from the same bolt of cloth," Hitchcock said. "I mean the original Charles Coborn, not the Hollywood one, whose name is spelled slightly different. The first Charles Coborn, who was famed for singing 'The Man That Broke the Bank at Monte Carlo,' attended the wartime funeral of another comedian named Harry Tate, who'd been hit by some antiaircraft-shell fragments. A large assembly of comedians was gathering at the graveside. Old Charles was so ancient that he was retired, and as the coffin was being lowered into the grave, one curious young sprout leaned over and whispered, 'How old are you, Charlie?'

" 'Eighty-nine,' Coborn said.

" 'Hardly seems worthwhile your going home,' the young 'un said.

"People constantly ask me, 'Why are you so interested in crime?' " Hitchcock went on. "The truth is I'm not. I'm only interested in it as it affects my profession. Actually I'm quite terrified of policemen; so much so that in 1939, when I first came to America, I refused to drive a car, for fear a policeman would stop me and give me a ticket. The thought that if I drove I would face that possibility day after day frightened me horribly, for I can't bear suspense."

"To me," I said, "one of the all-time classic motion-picture scenes was that pair, sitting in a small station in a European city with all hell breaking loose in the world around them while their only concern was to find out what the cricket scores were back in England. As an American," I went on, "it was the quintessence of Britishness. Did the British think it thoroughly British too?"

"No," Hitchcock said. "They knew that it was merely a humorous exaggeration. Such things have been called the Hitchcock touch, but they're actually more than that. They're really examples of English humor based on carry-

Hitchcock, son of a London poulterer, began his career designing title cards for silent films. Above, Tippi Hedren gets thumbs-up approval in Marnie.

ing understatement to an absurd extreme.

I suppose you might call it the oblique approach to melodrama. Melodrama is the most highly colored form of storytelling. Its villains, heroes and heroines are usually played heavy-handedly and bumblefootedly. I approach it somewhat differently. I've never gone in for the creaking-door type of suspense. To me, murder by a babbling brook drenched in sunshine is more interesting than murder in a dark and noisome alley littered with dead cats and offal.

"My hero is always the average man to whom bizarre things happen, rather than vice versa. By the same token, I always make my villains charming and polite. It's a mistake to think that if you put a villain on the screen, he must sneer nastily, stroke his black mustache or kick a dog in the stomach. Some of the most famous murderers in criminology—men for whom arsenic was so disgustingly gentle that they did women in with blunt instruments—had to be charmers to get acquainted with the females they murdered. The really frightening thing about villains is their surface likableness.

"Part of the fascination of the true murder lies in the fact that most real-life murderers are very ordinary, very polite, even engaging. I've heard the complaint that a true murder lacks mystery. To me, suspense is immeasurably more potent than mystery, and having to read a fiction murder story through in order to find out what happened bores me.

"I've never used the whodunit technique, since it is concerned altogether with mystification, which diffuses and unfocuses suspense. It is possible to build up almost unbearable tension in a play or film in which the audience knows who the murderer is all the time, and from the very start they want to scream out to all the other characters in the plot, 'Watch out for So-and-So! He's a killer!' There you have real tenseness and an irresistible desire to know what happens, instead of a group of characters deployed in a human chess problem. For that reason I believe in giving the audience all the facts as early as possible."

I asked, "How would you handle a potential bomb explosion in one of your stories?"

"The point is to let the audience know where the bomb is, but not let the characters in my story know," he said. "For example, you and I are sitting here chatting. We needn't talk about death or anything of serious consequence, but if the audience knows that there's a bomb under my desk, set to go off, the suspense will be harrowing to them. But if we don't tell our audience about the bomb ticking away under my desk, and it goes off and blows us to smithereens, the only thing the audience will get is a shock, and a one-second shock at that, as opposed to sixty to ninety minutes of breath-holding waiting."

I said I had heard that he had a reputation as an outstanding practical joker. "I have pretty much outgrown that now," he said. "And I'm afraid that if I tried to describe them to you, they'd seem pretty flat and contrived, but I still have a little fun in elevators. Sometimes in a crowded elevator I turn to someone with me and say, 'Of course, I didn't know the gun was loaded, but when it went off it blasted a great hole in his neck. A flap of his flesh fell down, and I could see the white ligaments uncovered. Presently I felt wetness around my feet. I was standing in a pool of blood.' Everyone stiffens; then I get out and leave them standing there."   *(1957)*

Merlin of the Movies

by Henry A. Reese

Orson Welles called him "the best makeup man in the world." Later, after doing without him for a short time, he changed his estimate. "You aren't the best makeup man in the world!" he roared. "You're the only makeup man in the world!"

Maurice Seiderman did all the character makeup for *Citizen Kane*. He molded Welles into thirty-seven phases of the name character. He subtly aged his face, his head, his neck, his hands, his body, even the irises of his eyes. He did it with a three-dimensional type of makeup which is at once the most effective and most difficult.

He spent three painstaking months with Welles before he was ready to apply any of the synthetic, and when it was ready it included six dozen different chins, ears, cheeks, jowls, hairlines, eye pouches. There were, for instance, sixteen different chins, and Welles never once appears in the picture with his own bare nose hanging out.

The hands became ridged with veins, the knuckles knobby and arthritic. And out of sight, the weight of the older Kane's body was also molded synthetic. With a coat of grease-paint the sagging breast line, pulpy paunch and little roll across the shoulders could have been shown naked—fleshy and normal, and right out of Seiderman's bottles.

The cement that holds the synthetic in place is another secret out of Maurice's bottles. His cement is so strong that if you were to clap a coated hand to your cheek you'd remove skin getting it away again. This is painful, so at the end of a working day Seiderman injects a hypodermic of solvent under the synthetic, the cement is dissolved, and off drops a double chin.

Despite the cement, Welles suddenly began losing pieces of face at odd moments. He fixed guilt on Welles. "You haff caught colt!" he complained, grabbed Welles by the chin, squeezed out a bit of perspiration, and vanished into his sanctum. Next day Welles was again a man of cohesive parts. Seiderman had analyzed his perspiration, found an increased acidity in Welles' body chemistry and prepared a new cement to meet the new condition.

Then, for as long as twenty-seven hours at a stretch, after spending three or four hours from four in the morning being made up, Welles worked with never a falling chin

or nose askew. The permanence of Seiderman's work is not its only advantage over other types of "rubber" makeup. Welles has as many allergies as talents, but Seiderman's synthetic caused no rashes or burns. According to actors who have suffered his and other artists' ministrations, his work is a marvel of comfort and gentleness.   *(1942)*

Part of the exquisite detail of Maurice's makeup included minutely reproducing Welles' skin, pore by pore, in plastic so that it would realistically absorb and diffuse light.

I Make Up Hollywood

by Wally Westmore

De Mille's Biblical extravaganza involved the use of more gallons of body makeup, more hundreds of yards of crepe hair and more people in front of movie cameras than any previous film. Body makeup is liquid made of dry color mixed with rose water and glycerin, and using three basic colors.

I lined up a battery of seven air-operated spray guns, and body makeup was sprayed on hundreds of extras in two spray booths—one booth for women, the other for men.

It was like a Detroit assembly line. The extras came into the studio, went to wardrobe, took off their clothes, hung them on racks, went into the spray booths, got sprayed, came out and were dried by big electric driers.

Two windows in our two spray booths overlooked the Hollywood cemetery. We sprayed hundreds of people every morning, and the fans sucked the mist of leftover body makeup out into the cemetery. One day A. C. Zoulis, the Paramount Studio's head engineer, called me on the phone and said, "I've just had a call from the Hollywood cemetery. They complain that their tombstones have turned brown and they can't wash them off."

Zoulis sent studio laborers with full buckets of detergent to scrub each gravestone, and my next move was to have big canvas flumes made, attach them to the fans and run those flumes down to the ground to guide the spray there.

I once found myself in a puzzling situation with Jack Benny's polar bear, Carmichael. Carmichael had become a familiar figure on the Benny radio program. So Paramount rented a polar bear, but for some reason his fur, instead of being white, was a dirty yellowish-brown. Probably smog-exposure. I said confidently, "We'll bleach him."

I mixed a bucket of bleach made of peroxide and ammonia, plus white powder, and gave it to the bear's trainer. The peroxide was twenty-volume peroxide—the strongest—and the ammonia made it work faster. Four days later my telephone was ringing. It was the bear's

According to Westmore, the female lead in **Lassie Come Home** *was played by a male Collie through the judicious application of makeup.*

trainer. He was screaming unintelligible threats.

"My bear!" he said. "No hair! No hair!"

It seems that bears are like dogs; their skin differs from human skin in that it has no pores. Everybody connected with the picture asked, "What are we going to do?" The only thing I could think of was to send for a supply of white crepe wool and have it glued over the bear's eroded areas. Before we were through, our animal looked like a white wool muff. *(1956)*

Edith and the 7 Oscars

by C. Robert Jennings

"A designer," says Edith Head, "is only as good as the star who wears her clothes." The reverse is also true. As boss designer of Paramount Pictures since 1938, Miss Head has reinforced the allure of some of the cinema's most spectacular stars.

"There was never an actress with whom it was easy to work," she says. "I have yet to see one completely unspoiled star, except for the animals—like Lassie. Each thinks she knows more than I do about her bust and hips." As a

result, she sees designing in Hollywood as a mixed drink: roughly one part style-savvy to three parts diplomacy, shaken with unrelenting psychoanalysis.

Through Edith Head's "clinic"—which is what she calls her elegant, silver-gray salon at Paramount—have paraded the most glamorous patients in the world. Clara Bow, she remembers, insisted on high heels for a celluloid game of tennis. And *She Done Him Wrong* brought Edith eyelet to eyelet with Mae (38-24-38) West. "I love fabric I can feel, honey," husked Mae. "So do men." When Edith showed her pictures of period jewelry, Mae said, "Fine, honey, just make the rocks *bigger*. Without diamonds, honey, I'd feel undressed." And to Edith's staff she purred, "I like 'em tight, girls." So they jammed Mae into costumes, says Edith, in which she could not "lie, bend or sit."

Miss Head remembers Hedy Lamarr spent "a good part of each fitting on the horizontal"; that Paulette Goddard toted her jewels around in a cigar box; and Betty Hutton made each fitting into a little show and brought along her own audience. Like Scarlett O'Hara, Liz Taylor had a 19-inch waist but always wanted her gowns "smaller, smaller." Juliet Prowse made things easy—"You just put the minimum of beads on the maximum of chassis," says Edith.

Most meticulous clothes horse in Hollywood, according to Edith, is not a woman at all, but Cary Grant. He plans an entire color scheme for his wardrobe, usually built around his leading lady's. And he wasn't very happy the day Sophia Loren's 14-karat gold dress rubbed off on his tux in a *Houseboat* clinch. Recalls Edith, "We had to spray her with lacquer so she would stay gold."

Miss Head's own influence on fads and fashion has extended beyond Hollywood. She launched a Latin-American trend with Barbara Stanwyck in *The Lady Eve*. Her sarong for Dorothy Lamour became a kind of institution— though Dottie was so unchesty it had to be taped on. Edith created Veronica Lake's half-nymph, half-witch look, and Audrey Hepburn's "Sabrina neckline," which had ties on each shoulder.   *(1963)*

Head-on confrontation. Edith did Grace Kelly's clothes in Hitchcock's Rear Window. *Jimmy Stewart wore a chic plaster cast; Grace was dressed like a fashion editor.*

"Let's face it," says Edith Head, "the public loves images. It's the actors who often resent being forever typed. Clothes are part of the image."

Picture Perfect
by Palma Wayne

"Dekko," says a maharaja in far-off India, "they have wrapped a high-caste turban on a low-caste houseboy."

"Look," snorts the American boy ironically, "guns didn't fire through the propeller on planes built that year."

And that is why the technical adviser was born. In Hollywood he is a psychologist, a mechanical adjunct to the picture, a living encyclopedia and a person who not alone saves his studio thousands of dollars but, what is more important, "face."

There are hundreds of different crafts shown daily in motion pictures throughout the world, and every individual belonging to one of them is waiting like a dog with a

bone, to pounce on their inaccuracies.

Here in Hollywood is where specialized knowledge at last has come into its own. Picture audiences have become more demanding in the validity of their screen fare. On the opening night of *A Farewell to Arms*, in New York, a distinguished surgeon chuckled under his breath during one of its most dramatic moments and said: "This is supposed to be an operating room in a war hospital in Italy in the front lines. Look over at the instruments on that table—most of them are maternity ones."

Well, what difference does it make, one asks. What's the odds whether the arrows in *Robin Hood* were made thirty-six inches long and those in medieval days measured forty-five inches, 2,000 arrows had to be remade? What's the odds whether a sequence in *The Charge of the Light Brigade* had to be retaken at a $50,000 added expense because in the "Charge" riders threw their lances and so disarmed themselves?

Just this: it is to these precise observances that we owe the reconstruction of the past, that makes it convincing. These minutiae give us the ability to hear things with our eyes.

In this screen kingdom, where the amount of money spent on research equals that expended by any scientific foundation in the world, arrived a few months ago the strangest pair of technical advisers ever to come to Hollywood. They both bore about them indications of small-town existence, but in the assembled knowledge permanently stored away in their minds, David Selznick has placed the welfare of *Gone With the Wind*. They are next-door neighbors and close friends of Margaret Mitchell, and their names are Mr. and Mrs. Wilbur Kurtz.

"Mr. Kurtz, props wants to know what the telegraph forms looked like"—and he goes over to his files and hands out an original, sent in 1862.

On the set with the director, Mrs. Kurtz is in close conference over the tying of the head rag on Mammy's head. "You'll have to take off that colored handkerchief. You see, she's a house servant and they only wore white ones—only yard and plantation slaves wore the colored bandannas. And be careful how it's tied—the ends are tucked under in the back. They never wore it with little rabbit ears stuck up in front—never."   *(1939)*

From duplicating uniforms to providing a replica of an 1862 telegraph form, Wilbur Kurtz supplied the knowledge that made **GWTW** *so historically believable.*

Lovely Loner

by Frank Condon

If all the strange people who recently have tried to talk to Greta Garbo were laid end to end, it would still be all right with the leading lady, especially if the people were surrounded with burial candles and the odor of incense. The West Coast pastime of trying to step up to Garbo becomes more fascinating day by day, and the strong, monastic veil that surrounds the heroine of Culver City has no weak spots or peek holes. Movie fans all over America spend considerable time wondering what she is like in the quiet surroundings of the home, and so do the residents of Hollywood, who, so to speak, live next door.

Because, so 'tis said, she dieted too rigidly at the start, her health was none too good and she has had to fight off the threat of anemia. That is why she takes those famous sun baths. She has a fine faith in the curative rays of the California sun, and has her sun bath daily, weather and the studio job permitting. And this sun-bath predilection is what started a small commotion and gave the studio a couple of frightened half hours.

An energetic young gentleman with a camera and a pad of paper made up his mind to crash through the barricades and acquire for himself a fine pot of money and deathless fame. He had heard tell of the sun baths and, selecting a rosy hour when the sun was high in the famous heavens of California, he descended upon the Santa Monica neighborhood where Garbo then lived. Carrying his camera carefully under his right arm, he came upon the thick hedge that protected the star from her public, and upon burrowing awhile, he perceived that the stories about Garbo taking sun baths were quite true; for lo and behold, there she was in person and, as you might say, in a highly epidermoidal state, happily taking her sun bath.

Pushing brambles and hedge blossoms aside, the bold fellow aimed his camera, took a picture of the famous sun bather, and then stood up beside the hedge to hear if the lady had anything to say, indicating he would be glad to jot it down. The astounded Garbo wrapped her suntan up in a blanket and bade the young marauder to get him gone, and her commands of the moment were sprinkled with viking words referring to heat and brimstone.

The visitor wrote down what he could remember of the conversation, crawled backward through the hedge and later announced that he had, for cash sale to publications, a brisk statement by Miss Greta Garbo, and one (1) photograph of a rather interesting character, showing a lady alone with her sun. When the studio heard that a young man was walking up and down Hollywood Boulevard with a photograph, there was quite a bit of telephoning, but the alarums were groundless.

When the stolen photo was sold, developed and studied, it was a complete failure. The only living thing in it was the Garbo cat. Over in the corner devoted to sun bathing, there was nothing but a formless blob, and everybody in California breathed a sigh of relief. *(1932)*

She was fire; she was ice. She was intelligent, superbly talented, breathlessly beautiful. Some call her performance in the 1936 Camille *"the greatest on film." Her co-star: young Robert Taylor. Few left the theater dry-eyed after her death scene at the film's end.*

Cary On

by Pete Martin

An old Hollywood saying goes: "They'd buy the telephone book as a story for Bing Crosby or Ingrid Bergman if they thought either of them would play in it."

RKO didn't buy a story based on the telephone book for Cary Grant. But it did something else for him almost as incredible.

Charlie Koerner, then RKO's general manager, was aprowl for a story to use as bait in luring Grant into making a picture for him. He was stirring up his story department with a big stick. He was wooing those agents who had authors' wares for sale. Busily he was reappraising the story properties RKO had bought, but had never used.

Grant happened to speak favorably to someone of a

book called *None But the Lonely Heart*. Such things get bruited around the film capital with the mysterious rapidity of native tom-tom. Koerner heard of it, rushed out and bought the story. Selecting a phone from among the nest of those clustered on his desk, he called producer David Hempstead.

"I want you to get set to make a picture, Dave," he said.

"What is this picture I'm to make?" Hempstead asked.

Koerner replied enthusiastically, "*None But the Lonely Heart*. Grant likes it. I've just paid sixty thousand dollars for it."

Hempstead, a normally cautious man, inquired with mild irony, "I don't want to seem the prying type, but just what is the story all about?"

Koerner confessed that he didn't know, that he hadn't read it. He suggested that they get together, call Grant and ask him to give them a quick takeout on the plot.

Once they had Grant on the phone, Koerner said, "Well, Cary, we've bought that story for you, but I'm a little vague about the story line and I want you to give Dave here a brief résumé of it."

"What story?" Grant asked.

"*None But the Lonely Heart*," Koerner replied.

"I haven't read it," Grant told him. "A friend of mine told me he thought it good. That's all I know about it."

So, as if to prove that Hollywood is—in fact as well as in fiction—a blend of Aladdin's wonderful lamp and Stephen Leacock's Nonsense Novels come true, Grant played in this story, bought for him without anyone at RKO having read it. To compound the miracle further, it scored a critical success.

It was a generous fairy godmother who hovered over the cradle in Bristol, England, on January 18, 1904, when a male child, afterward to be known as Cary Grant, was born to Elias and Lillian Leach. The name the couple selected for the child was Archibald Alexander Leach. Upon the red-faced infant, born with a fuzz of jet-black hair upon his bullethead, she bestowed a quality that was afterward to stand him in good stead in his chosen profession. Now, in the midst of Hollywood's present panics and alarums, it is a quality that bids fair to keep him from joining those stars who are tumbling downward with a falling box office.

British-born Cary (shown here in **Father Goose***) ran away from home at 11 to join an acrobatic troupe. The name* **Cary** *came from a play role,* **Grant** *from the phone book.*

"No great shakes as an actor but he has a certain niftiness,"
said an early critic. That quality has worn well.

That quality is being able to climb down from the screen, get inside of a fan's skin, walk out into the street inside of him and stay there for a while after the lights have flickered on in a palace of the cinema.

Cary Grant holds the all-time record for being many times the Academy of Motion Picture Arts and Sciences' bridesmaid, but never its blushing bride. In 1937, Leo McCarey won an Academy Award for directing *The Awful Truth*. In 1940 an award went to James Stewart for his part in *The Philadelphia Story*. In 1941 Joan Fontaine was tapped for her portrait of the fear-ridden girl in *Suspicion*. Ethel Barrymore took home an Oscar in 1944 as the mother in *None But the Lonely Heart*. In all these films Grant was the big attraction. He was not the big prize winner.

Being just himself in films, however, has given Grant no case of box-office anemia. In the nationwide Box-Office poll of top male stars for 1948, he ranked fourth. He was topped only by the seemingly perpetual trio of Crosby, Cooper and Gable. The premiere of *The Bishop's Wife* was accompanied by critical hosannas. But when it accomplished nothing startling at the box office, Sam Goldwyn, its producer, retitled it *Cary and the Bishop's Wife*. Injecting Grant's first name into the billing upped the film's business as much as 25 percent.

It also proved that Grant belongs to the small company of those human beings whose first names are readily recognized by large chunks of the public without the help of any other identification.

While his fairy godmother's gift is the keystone of Grant's screen appeal, it is more complex than that gift alone indicates. Queried about the Grant appeal, a studio messenger girl offered this slant: "He's got finesse. And he's sophisticated. His charm is boyish, only it's kind of mature. Of course, the fact that he's tall, good-looking and has a cleft chin doesn't hurt any."

Mike Curtiz, the Hungarian director who talks in such a surrealistic way that his conversation has been hailed as a whole new language, once said of Grant, "Some actors squeeze a line to death. Cary tickles it to life."

When most stars hit the heights they think they're magic. They have a notion that anything they do is right. Not Grant. It's his conviction that it's up to him to find out what people like in Grant; what they expect of him. Then do it. Many Hollywood stars don't see their own pictures. If they do, it's usually in the plush-insulated solitude of a studio projection room. Grant sees each of his films in the regular-run movie houses. He studies the reactions of different audiences. If one of his pieces of stage business or one of his gestures rings the bell, it's apt to be in his next picture two or three times.

Grant quit Paramount because he felt that "playing all the parts Gary Cooper didn't want" was unsatisfactory. When Columbia signed him for $75,000 a year, Hollywood thought that studio had taken leave of its wits. Its

opinion changed when Grant was cast in *The Awful Truth*. In this, his first smash hit, a not-too-low comedy, he was called upon to portray married devotion with a touch of humor. It meant being gay, brave, and elegant in absurd situations. Then getting out of those situations as neatly as a pin. In short, he conducted himself in exactly the way all husbands feel that they probably conduct themselves if only the truth were known.

An analogy he has worked out between Hollywood and a streetcar fascinates Grant. The analogy had its genesis in a Charlie Chaplin comedy. In that comedy Chaplin was a part of a queue waiting to board a streetcar. He got into the car first all right, but there were so many in line that they pushed him on through the car and he fell out the other end. Getting to his feet, he ran around, climbed on again and hung on as best he could.

As Grant sees it, Hollywood is that streetcar. "The car just goes around in circles, not going anywhere," he says. "There is room on it for just so many, and every once in a while, if you look back, you'll see that someone has fallen off to let a new passenger on. When Ty Power got on, it meant we left someone sprawled out on the street; and somebody had to fall off to make room for Greg Peck. Some fellows who get pushed off run around and climb back on as character actors. Adolphe Menjou is one. Ronald Colman sits up with the motorman. And Gary Cooper is smart. He never gets up to give anybody his seat. After much confusion and waiting, I finally got a seat. But I lost it temporarily when I got up to make room for a young lady named Joan Fontaine, who co-starred with me in *Suspicion* and won an Oscar in that movie. So there I am, just standing up, hanging onto a strap, and being jostled around." *(1949)*

Lord Larry

by Sam Walton

At the Pinewood Studios near London, producer Morton Gottlieb is making *Sleuth* with Laurence Olivier and Michael Caine. Outside, a leaden English sky causes cameramen to praise and aging actresses to curse the power of artificial lighting in the studio's 141,000 square feet.

Sir Laurence (his correct term of address is now the Honorable Lord Olivier, but he prefers "Sir" to "Lord") is sixty-five. His fans, knowing the ways of this world, would not be surprised to see the face that has settled on the man is not the face of the melancholy Dane or the passionate Heathcliff, but that of Archie Rice in *The Entertainer* ("The role I was happiest in")—tough, enduring, the businessman (the business of staying on top) rather than the

sensitive artist, which, of course, he is too. (See the National Theatre Company's *Three Sisters* and *The Merchant of Venice*.)

Olivier is wearing a soft shirt, open at the neck, the inevitable English ascot. His feet repose in velvet slippers, the monogram "A. W." (Andrew Wyke) emblazoned in gold. Dark-rimmed spectacles double the strength of his famous square chin. Nobody would deny—certainly not his third actress wife, Jean Plowright—that he is a handsome man. He talks about *Sleuth* with enthusiasm.

"I first saw it performed at Brighton." (His home, a beautiful Regency mansion.) "I was immensely impressed. Here was a head-on collision between a mature, cultivated man of letters, antagonistic towards the changed values of the time, and a younger man who represented those values. His brashness and confidence epitomized everything the older man despises."

It is not just the plot, though, that makes *Sleuth* exciting. Shade by shade (a pun intended) the characters of the two men are revealed. You are left to decide which is the deadlier. It is a tough decision. "Andrew is a man having a lifelong love affair with himself," says Olivier, considering for a moment his broad hands as if he were not especially unfond of himself, "and all this is threatened by the intrusion of Tindle, who is having a sexual affair with his wife. For Andrew this is far more than a triangular inconvenience. It is a terrible shattering of his self-esteem, the revelation of his fundamental impotence.

"Tony Shaffer has described Wyke as a man who has only his good taste left to bully others with. It is a very apt description because Wyke is a snob. But it is not the whole truth." For a moment, Olivier seems to assume the role with an eerie kind of exactness. "Wyke is a very polished snob with much to be snobbish about. He has talent, charm, wealth, refinement, and sophistication, and although some of those qualities may be dubious they are never dull. They shine in an increasingly average world."

"We play off each other perfectly," chimes in Caine. "We had never met, Olivier and I, before the first rehearsal. We're as different as people can be.

"There are masses of wonderful surfaces to bounce anything off that you want to. You bounce a table-tennis ball off his surface and it comes back a diamond." *(1972)*

*Olivier in Everyman's dream role, **Hamlet** (Best Movie, Best Actor 1948). Repertory theater background allowed him to bridge gap between romantic and character parts.*

Best Bette

From the moment I read *Dark Victory* I wanted to play Judith Traherne. Jack Warner felt that a picture about death would be too depressing, but I convinced him that this was a story of life, not death, because Judith learns that it isn't how long we live that's important, but how we live.

Judith was my kind; I respected and understood this girl who, at twenty-three, learned that she had only a few months to live. Although her background—money and the social whirl—differed from mine, I sympathized with her emotions and her way of thinking, her preference for the cold truth. She had the thoroughbred qualities we all admire. Here were the elements that make for a favorite role.

Bette with Henry Fonda in Jezebel *(1938). The movie's last scenes focused heavily on her—he'd left the set early to witness the birth of his daughter, Jane Fonda.*

Edmund Goulding, the director; George Brent, who played the doctor; Geraldine Fitzgerald in the part of Judith's friend Ann—all of us loved the story, and from that fact there came that wonderful feeling of reality and oneness which rarely happens on a Hollywood set. George and I had shared six other films, but I know this was both our best and our most important, our lucky seventh.

The most beautiful scene was the one where Judith, in the garden planting flowers that will bloom for the man she loves, suddenly realizes that the sunlight is not so brilliant as it should be, that she is going blind; and she quietly draws on a great courage to face the end. We had to do the scene again and again.

I knew there must be no tears, for Judith wouldn't have cried, but time after time I could not help crying. It was an unforgettable experience, portraying Judith's victory over the dark. *(1946)*

Iron Maiden
by Lupton A. Wilkinson and J. Bryan, III

The Warrior's Husband had been produced on a shoe-string. As a leading lady, Kate's salary had been only $100 a week, and this had been cut to $79.50 at the time she signed with Selznick. The effect of her $1,420.50-per-week raise, plus the other concessions, was precisely as might have been expected from someone of her psychology. She approached Hollywood with a thorough conviction that it was vulgar and flabby-minded.

Her friend Laura Harding came along on the "slumming trip."

Halfway to the Coast, they were sitting in the diner one night when Kate pointed through the window. "Look! New moon!"

Laura was alarmed. "That means bad luck, Kate! You ought never to see the new moon through glass!"

Kate laughed at her. After dinner they went to the rear platform. As Kate opened the door, something flew into her left eye. She thought it was a cinder, but she couldn't dislodge it. The eye began to swell.

Leland Hayward and his partner, Myron Selznick, met her train at Pasadena. They will never forget the sight. One of Kate's eyes was shut tight. The other was inflamed sympathetically. Her freckles seemed as big as potato

Kate and Cary in **The Philadelphia Story** *(1940). 1939 "Box-office Poison," she came back with 417 Broadway performances of this comedy, then made the movie.*

chips. She was wearing a bizarre blue suit and a pancake straw hat that in 1941 might be called "stylishly insane"; in 1932 it was merely insane. Red hair and eyes, white face, blue suit—the date was July 4, 1932.

"My God," Selznick whispered to Hayward. "Did we stick David fifteen hundred for *that*?"

The yellow Rolls-Royce in which she was driven to the studio struck Kate, on her part, "as an indication of what asses they must be in Hollywood, so I became 'refined.'"

Selznick tried to make conversation. "I understand you're quite a golfer. Did you bring your clubs?"

"I don't think I'll care to play out here," said Kate.

Selznick tried again. "Where are you going to stay?"

"Why do you want to know?" she asked.

"I don't," said Selznick angrily, "I was just being polite."

Not another word was spoken on the rest of the ride. The agents delivered the girls to David Selznick in silence and disappeared. Selznick, too, took a single look, then stepped into the next office and phoned Cukor. "*Your* star is here, George. I'll send her down."

Cukor had a sheaf of dress designs spread out. Still

Here with Bogie in The African Queen *(1951), she has a record eleven nominations as Best Actress (winning thrice).*

"busy being superior," Kate leafed through them contemptuously. Her only comment was, "Not quite the sort of thing a well-bred English girl would wear, I'm afraid."

"No?" said Cukor. "And what do you think of what you're wearing now?"

"I think it's very smart."

"Well, I think it stinks."

Fortunately, they were interrupted by the entrance of John Barrymore, whom she was to play opposite.

Kate liked him from the first.

"I'm so glad you're here," he said. "I saw your test, and I know you're going to be a big star."

Suddenly he leaned toward her and peered at her closely. His manner changed.

"Come into the hall," he told her.

She followed meekly. Barrymore gestured toward her eyes. "I have that same trouble once in a while myself," he said confidentially, taking a small bottle from his pocket, "but this stuff is marvelous. A couple of drops in each eye, and they'll never know you've been hitting it up."

"But, Mr. Barrymore," Kate said, "I have something in my eye."

Barrymore winked. "I know. I know." He put the bottle into her hand, patted her, and walked away. *(1941)*

All's Welles

by Alva Johnston and Fred Smith

Orson Welles, the boy who raised gooseflesh on a continent with his Martian monsters, received his first important publicity in 1925, when he was ten years old.

A newspaper of Madison, Wisconsin, printed a column about him in 1925 under the headline, A POET, ARTIST, CARTOONIST AND ACTOR AT 10 YEARS. The body of the article added that he was a writer, being the author of a tale entitled "The Yellow Panther." Although the article failed to mention it, Orson was also a dramatist and magician. He had written a play on how to run a hotel and could extract burning buildings from silk handkerchiefs.

The infant prodigy was particularly successful "in the art of makeup and impersonations," according to the article, which added:

"At times when Orson is in the midst of a story and becomes particularly interested in one of the characters, he is seized with an inspiration to paint the character, and forthwith takes up his box of oil paints, making a study that, though it is amateurish in technique, shows a keen insight and appreciation."

The article was illustrated with a photograph of the many-sided little wizard. It is the face of a young Grand Lama with large slanting eyes and an air of profound Mongolian wisdom. Welles has not changed completely in the fourteen years since then; he can still act the part of a Chinese without makeup. There was a touch of precocious showmanship or premature ham in the newspaper photograph; the young maestro is almost lost in an enormous black silk scarf, draped about his throat in artist fashion. According to his guardian, Orson hunted up the Latin Quarter necktie the moment he learned that he was to have his picture in the paper. At ten years he was already abusing the simplicity of the public.

Orson was an old war horse in the infant-prodigy line by the time he was ten. He had already seen eight years' service as a child genius. The I-knew-him-when people in the Orson Welles circle recall vividly that at two he talked like a college professor and looked like The Mysterious Dr. Fu Manchu. Devout people were inclined to cross themselves in the presence of the eerie little being. Some of the oldest acquaintances of Welles have been disappointed in his career. They see the twenty-four-year-old boy of today as a mere shadow of the two-year-old man they used to know. Granted that he has attracted some attention as an actor, director, producer, designer, writer, radio star, Shakespearean editor and continent scarer, they neverthe-

less consider him a hollow shell of his former self. He is thought to be going backward, like the Scott Fitzgerald hero who was born at seventy and retrogressed to zero.

The most puzzled people in the United States on Sunday night, October 30, 1938, were the traffic policemen of New Jersey. There were plenty of frightened citizens in America at that time, but the most confused ones were the motorcycle cops on the highways between New York and Philadelphia. At about 8:15 or 8:20 p.m. most of the traffic over those roads suddenly went wild.

Hundreds of automobiles began to flash along at speeds which normally indicate gangsters leaving scenes of assassination. But there were family parties in most of the cars; the women and children couldn't all be gun molls and child racketeers. When a motorcycle man tried to overhaul one speeding auto, he was passed by two or three others. The stampede was in all directions. Nobody would stop for a policeman's hail. Now and then, a traffic man would catch an incoherent shout that there was an "invasion" or that "the world was coming to an end."

There were puzzled policemen in station houses all over the country, as demands came over the telephone for gas masks and information as to the safest places to hide from the enemy. The second most puzzled group were the switchboard operators, as the telephones suddenly went crazy and began to rave deliriously. Next came the clergy; priests were startled by the rush to get confessions under the wire, and Protestant ministers astonished at the interruption of their sermons by demands for prayers to avert the impending doom of the world. Fourth in the order of puzzlement may well have been hospital attendants who were called on to handle the nervous wrecks and falling-downstairs cases.

The puzzled section of the population was slow in discovering the cause of the panic, because the panic-stricken people had different stories to tell. They had tuned in at different periods during the Columbia network's broadcast of the "invasion" and had many different ideas about the invaders. Some said they were octopus-like Martian monsters armed with poison gas and death rays. Others thought it was merely the world coming to an end, as per schedule. Others identified the invaders as Germans; still others, as Japanese. Princeton sociologists, who interviewed victims of the panic in the interests of science, found one man who had thought the invaders were Chinese.

Welles in Citizen Kane, *the movie based on William Randolph Hearst. The film infuriated Hearst, who forbade his newspapers to run reviews or advertise it.*

The wonder boy had broken loose again. Orson Welles, the child wizard, had had another brainstorm. After having Harlemized and gangsterized Shakespeare, he had decided to put Orson Welles effects into the solar system. The twenty-three-year-old earth shaker had taken *The War of the Worlds*, an old-fashioned thriller written by H. G. Wells in 1898, and given it a modern treatment, using a combination of newscast and newspaper styles. His success in scaring the nation resulted from the capable handling of the old familiar earmarks of credibility. He gave names, addresses, occupations and other minute details; identified each farm, hamlet, turnpike, knoll, swamp and creek in the terrain which the Martian monsters swept over; christened every cop and village loafer who got mixed up in the interplanetary unpleasantness.

It was this change of pace from the particular to the cosmic that paralyzed the reasoning powers of his listeners. The seasoning of little facts of geography and personal identity caused the Welles public to swallow his wildest absurdities.

According to the Gallup poll, 9 million people heard all or part of the Martian broadcast; according to the estimate of the Princeton sociologists, approximately 1.75 million people were frightened. At any rate, while Welles was grinding away at what he apparently considered an intolerably dull routine, strange things were happening around the country, samples of which are as follows:

Public-spirited citizens of Providence, Rhode Island, telephoned to the local utility demanding a blackout. A Pittsburgh woman tried to drink poison, saying, "I'd rath-er die this way than like that." A linotyper of Selma, Louisiana, running in the dark, caught his chin under a neighbor's clothesline and thought he was hit by a death ray. A Mobile woman, getting the news on returning from the Greater Mobile Gulf Coast Fair, said to her husband, "I had a premonition that we should have gone to church instead of the fair." A colored woman, later interviewed by the Princeton sociologists, recalled that there was half a chicken left in the icebox, and said, "We might as well eat it now, because we won't be here in the morning." The staff of the *Memphis Press-Scimitar* rushed to the office to get out an extra. Misled by neon lights in the distance and by the gasoline-and-rubber fumes on the highways, many residents of New Jersey claimed to have seen and smelled the Martians, who were supposed to have landed near Princeton. A man ran into the Press Club at Princeton University saying that he had seen the Martian spaceship explode and had observed animals jumping from it. The town of Concrete, Washington, got a double dose of terror, as the local power-and-light plant broke down just as Orson Welles was saying that the poison gas was choking him.

The chief victim of the panic is Welles himself. He is branded for life as the Mars man. People bear down on him like 10,000 Ancient Mariners on one wedding guest and hold him while he listens to their Martian stories. He can detect a glitter in the eye of every stranger; from the nature of the glitter, he can figure to the split second how long it will be before the stranger comes over and opens a Martian conversation. Welles sees on nearly everybody a burning time fuse which at a given moment is going to burst into a Martian epigram or question. He is a pathetic figure today. *(1940)*

Wild Old West

by Lewis Lapham

At the age of 71 Miss West still possesses overwhelming sexual force. It comes and goes, like distant music heard across a fairgrounds on a summer night, but it is there.

She received us in her bedroom, seated on a gold chair in front of her round bed. Over a pink satin nightgown of the type preferred by movie stars of the 1930s she wore a negligee of fine lace. Her corsets held her figure rigidly in place. She wore a long, blond wig and exaggerated false eyelashes. The only sure marks of her age were the deep wrinkles in her throat and the lines around her eyes and wrists.

"How are ya?" she said, grandly extending her hand.

She wasted no time with the customary preliminaries,

assuming that if I had come up to see her then I must be interested in only one subject.

"With me," she began, "sex has always been a natural thing, part of my personality, you know what I mean?"

I nodded in numb agreement.

"My basic style I never changed, but I've always had a dignity and a regalness. Half the women in the world have copied me. I stimulated 'em. Those other actresses, those imitators, who are they? What have they done? Who heard of 'em? They just walk around on a stage lookin' dirty. Where's the humor? Where's the laugh in back of it?"

"Nowhere," I eagerly agreed, "no laugh, nothing but common drabs tricked up in tight skirts."

"Young man," she said, "I see you understand a few things. I used to go for guys with fancy rings, or a watch fob, or a natty suit, but I learned to be more particular.

"I was the first person to bring sex out into the open. Before I came along nobody could even print the word on billboards. I was walkin' on the West Side in New York one day with a certain party when I saw a girl in a satin dress wearing a ninety-eight-cent hat and feathers from a bird of paradise. A low and vulgar girl accompanied by sailors, but the feathers were worth a lot of money at the time, being, of course, illegal. So I said to the party I was with, where did that girl get that bird of paradise? I figured she got 'em from the sailors, who must have smuggled 'em into the country. That was the inspiration for my play, *Sex*. A catchy title and the basis of all life."

To demonstrate my good intentions and remove any taint of suspicion, I asked, in my most literary style, whether in these modern and degenerate times anybody still played the great game between the sexes with the old grace and charm, or whether, like the language of ancient Crete, the art of love had disappeared without a trace. She replied that here and there (her dispirited gesture summoned up visions of haggard soldiers holding out in lonely bunkers against heavy tanks) a few players still observed the old rules.

"But with most of 'em it's like handin' over a package of cigarettes. Sex is like a small business; you gotta protect it, watch over it. A matter of timing.

"The score never interested me," she said, "only the game."   *(1964)*

The infinite Miss West fields an approach shot from that great devotee of dogs and children, W. C. Fields, in My Little Chickadee *(1940). Critics called it a draw.*

Glamorous Grandma

by Stanley Frank

For fifteen years Gloria Swanson's contract had been one of the most valuable properties in the movie industry, but after 1934 no studio wanted any part of it. Producers had polite evasions—"The only thing open is too small for you, darling"—and elaborate excuses—"I'm working on a reduced budget and I wouldn't dream of asking you to cut your price"—but the double-talk added up to a blunt verdict: she was washed up. Her comeback in *Sunset Boulevard* does not prove the producers were wrong. It demonstrates, rather, that the sophisticated, chichi stereotype she had been playing since 1919 was wrong for audiences struggling through the depression. Once she knew she was finished, Miss Swanson left Hollywood without the parting blast at the business that is standard operating procedure for disgruntled stars.

She realized that her time had run out when, in the fall of 1938, her appearance on the streets of Paris no longer aroused a small riot.

Getting the brush-off from Hollywood was just a glancing blow compared to the shock Miss Swanson got when she realized that most of her money was gone. It seems incredible that a woman whose average annual income was three quarters of a million dollars for a decade would have to worry about money, but Miss Swanson's extravagances had been just as incredible.

Miss Swanson had a go at all existing free-style records for spending. On her first trip to Europe in 1924, she engaged the Prince of Wales suite on the S.S. *Berengaria*. In Paris, she rented the Marquise de Bront's six-story town house and a staff of bewigged flunkies in satin knee breeches. Among other creature comforts, the house had a master bathroom with a large sunken tub. Flanking the tub were a pair of massive stone urns whose function mystified Miss Swanson until she was told they were for wafting fragrance through the bathroom. She ordered the most expensive Paris perfume for the urns. Weeks later she learned it was customary, even among the bon ton, to fill the urns with tap water and drop in scented powder which could be bought for a franc at any pharmacy.

"One day my mother was out for a walk with Gloria on

Fifth Avenue," Mrs. Jane Walton, her former press representative, relates. "There was an emerald necklace as big as a dog collar in the window of Cartier's, and Gloria went in to price it. She didn't bat an eye when she was told it was $50,000. She was about to buy it when my mother steered her to a star-sapphire ring that cost only $5,000. Mother acted as though diverting Gloria from the necklace was a feat comparable to converting a tribe of head-hunters, and if you knew Gloria, it was." *(1950)*

After 50 years in the movies, Swanson flashes her famous smile. "Health food and hard work," she explains.

General Jim
by Pete Martin

Lou Wasserman, of the Music Corporation of America, is a man who is famed in the flesh-peddling business for his chilled-steel aplomb. The M.C.A. is just about the largest handler of entertainment talent in the world. As one of its key men, Wasserman is a driver of hard bargains. The pounds of flesh plus blood that he has exacted for his clients have left many a movie director and producer whimpering into their hand-painted neckties. But on one occasion the imperturbable Wasserman was flabbergasted. Never in all his bargaining days had he been asked to insert a clause in an actor's contract which remotely resembled the one demanded by the thin, gawky man slouched on the far side of his desk.

In a voice whose high-pitched and hesitant qualities are known to movie audiences everywhere, Jimmy Stewart was outlining the one condition upon which he would star in a film Frank Capra planned to make. With his lower lip protruding and a lock of hair tumbling down over his forehead in a fashion that would have been affectionately recognized by millions of fans, he reread the clause he insisted upon. "In all advertising and publicity issued by the corporation, or under its control," it specified, "the corporation will not mention or cause to be mentioned the

The great Kate lights up for an apprehensive Stewart, the quintessential inarticulate shy guy, in **The Philadelphia Story** *(1940) remade in 1956 as a musical,* **High Society.**

They say Ziegfeld glorified the American girl and New York wore her over its heart like an orchid. In Ziegfeld Girl *Lana Turner played the orchid, Jimmy her beau.*

part taken by the artist in World War II as an officer in the U.S. Army."

That clause was one of a series of efforts the actor had made to keep Jimmy Stewart, movie star, and Col. James Maitland Stewart, of the 8th Air Force, separate and distinct. During his early days in the Army, the efforts of various Air Force public-relations officers to hitch their publicity wagons to his stardom had eaten into his soul. Now that he was back in civilian clothes he was grimly determined that no studio publicist should switch that pitch and cash in on his Army record. As Major (later Colonel) James Maitland Stewart, he had led more than 1,000 heavy bombers on a strike aimed at a vital German war-plant target.

Stewart's fight to be treated like any other soldier had begun in 1941, when the news got back to Metro-Goldwyn-Mayer, the studio to which he was under contract, that he'd tried to enlist, only to be turned down as underweight. M-G-M told him, "Relax. We'll try to fix it so you won't be drafted." It had made him furious. He rented a 400-h.p. plane, paid for it at seventeen dollars an hour out of his own pocket, spent 200 flying hours learning to be a pilot. To put the minimum amount of padding on his bones required by Army regulations, he ate spaghetti twice a day and stuffed himself with other fattening foods.

One of Stewart's closest friends is the Metro-Goldwyn-Mayer executive, Billy Grady. Man and boy, Grady has been connected with show business throughout most of his long life and, as a stage and movie old-timer, he is apt to talk as if reading a scenario. "Jimmy goes down for his next physical," Grady said, "and I'm there to take him in a studio car. He refuses to go in a limousine. He goes by trolley instead, and leaves me standing there with egg on my face. I tail him to the place where they look Army candidates over. I sit there waiting. When a medical officer comes out, I ask him if Jim has made it. 'He's made it by one ounce,' the officer says. What that officer doesn't know is that Jim is so determined to make the weight that he hasn't been to the bathroom for thirty-six hours. It's been torture, but it puts him over."

It is difficult to decide where Stewart the screen actor ends and Stewart himself begins. The Stewart the public sees is Every Man; not Every Man of Distinction, but Every Average Man. Instinctively, audiences think of the screen Stewart as a product of a small American town and of God-fearing parents endowed with a saving sense of humor. It is impossible to think of the screen Stewart as egotistical or a braggart. It is equally hard to think of him as much concerned with sartorial matters. He seems far happier in a beat-up windbreaker than a business suit. "Your face and clothes look as if they'd been lived in," one fan wrote him. "I like them that way."

His delivery of dialogue is the reverse of glib. Apparently he is engaged in an endless struggle for and with words.

This struggle becomes especially noticeable when he plays opposite his leading lady of the moment. High or low voltaged, blonde, brunette or redhead, their presence appears to render him awkward, shy, inarticulate.

In private, as well as in such screen characterizations as his portrayal of Elwood Dowd in *Harvey*, Stewart conveys the impression of being relaxed. His conversation is geared to the poky pace of a cracker-barrel philosopher. So thoroughly has he mastered the art of slowing talk down that he once managed to carry on a conversation with another non-wordy man, Gary Cooper, without conversing at all. He was standing in front of his house when Cooper drove up, pulled over to the curb and opened his car door. Jimmy climbed in and Cooper made shooting gestures with his hands. Jimmy nodded and got out. Nothing had been said; nevertheless, an invitation to go hunting had been made and accepted.

Having remained single so long, Jimmy had trouble getting used to being a family man. During the first few weeks after his marriage, when he started for the studio he forgot the time-honored husbandly custom of a good-bye kiss. En route to work, he'd remember that he was married, duck into a phone booth, call his wife and say contritely, "Good-bye, dear."

Told by an obstetrician that he was to become the father of twins, he went into a tailspin of new worriments and brooded about whether he would be able to find the shortest possible route to the maternity hospital when the time came to rush his wife there. He decided to make a dry run, clocking himself with a stop watch as he drove. So closely did he keep his eyes glued on the split-second hand that he got lost, and was able to complete his journey only with directions from a filling-station attendant.   *(1951)*

Phantom Star

by Pete Martin

The public has been taught to think of Hollywood as a Bedlam on the Wilshire where studio executives toss money around as casually as urchins playing with beanbags. The truth is that, when it comes to getting a studio its money's worth, movie executives are as canny as Yankee peddlers. With Gregory Peck's advent, however, they trampled one another underfoot in their eagerness to lay out money for the services of a youngster most of them had never seen, even fleetingly, in a screen test. It was a 1944 Klondike gold rush. It was keeping up with the Joneses on a hundred-grand scale. "It was," as one participant put it, "murder." Another described it, "The news that there was somebody tall, dark and handsome, *who could also act*, on the other side of the mountains, seemed to get around by native tom-tom."

Suddenly, people previously regarded as sane were scrambling and snarling and begging for a piece of a young man who had made only one movie, *Days of Glory*, and that one hadn't been released, and nobody had seen it. He had been in three New York plays that were strictly morning-glories with an average run of about four weeks each. All anybody knew was that he, personally, had emerged from those flops with good notices.

Before the bidding and the finagling and the uproar had simmered down, parts of Peck belonged to four different studios, and his name was signed to contracts obligating him to eight years of celluloid servitude. Two of his first three starring roles, *The Keys of the Kingdom, The Valley of Decision* and *Spellbound*, were played opposite the tops in feminine acting talent—Ingrid Bergman and Greer Garson. And all this had happened to him before the public had seen a single foot of film in which his profile—a cross between a young, beardless Lincoln and the Gary Cooper of *A Farewell to Arms*—appeared.

One movie writer put it, "This time Hollywood, rather than the paying customers, can take credit for recognizing a gold mine when they saw the same." The emergence of Peck was even more miraculous than that. Hollywood had recognized a gold mine without having seen it at all.

Perhaps the best place to begin Peck's story is with a phone call received by his agent, Leland Hayward. Hayward has been around Hollywood a long time, and is not given to hysteria. His account of the Peck stampede, therefore, is all the more impressive.

The voice on the New York end of the wire belonged to Casey Robinson, a motion-picture writer who wanted to become a motion-picture producer. He was still working for Warner Brothers, but was just about to sever his connection with that studio. "You handle a boy named Peck," stated Robinson.

"Do I?" Hayward asked.

"You do," Robinson said. "I've just seen him in a show, and he's good. Hal Wallis is going to call you, too, to try to sign him for Warner Brothers, but I'm first. I want Peck exclusive."

"I didn't know what Casey was talking about," Hayward said. "I'd never heard of Peck. So I stalled. 'Of course, he'll want time off to appear in an occasional stage play,' I suggested."

That didn't faze Robinson, so Hayward took a deep breath, said, "He won't make tests, either," and waited for the outraged howls. But Robinson took that one in his stride too. Hayward began to mention things that were ordinarily like flapping red flags in a producer's face. "He must have approval of the first two or three pictures he does.... You can't sign him for more than three years.... He must get a thousand a week for his first picture, fifteen hundred for his second and two thousand for his third." He sat back and waited for the wires to melt as they carried Robinson's reply westward. But Robinson merely said "Okay," and hung up.

The phone rang again. This time it was Hal Wallis. Hayward went through his list of Peck-won't-do-this-and-Peck-won't-do-that again. They bothered Wallis no more than they had Robinson. Bill Goetz, then with Twentieth Century-Fox, phoned, and once more Hayward went through his Peck-is-hard-to-get routine. "Goetz wondered if I was nuts or something," Hayward said. " 'We don't sign actors to terms like that in these times,' he told me." But he capitulated too. Then Paramount called, and RKO. David Selznick had tested Greg in New York and had passed him up, but when the Peck fever seized him, he called Hayward and said, "The kid was very young then—I want him back again."

In desperation, Hayward took a plane to New York to see his mystery man in person. When Hayward told him, "I'll take you to the Coast and let you look them all over," the promise was symptomatic of the amazing way things were working out. Ordinarily he would have said, "I'll take you to the Coast and let them look *you* over."   *(1945)*

For Peck, **To Kill a Mockingbird** *and* **To Get an Oscar are the same. He has also gathered four other nominations.**

Mar-lay-nah
by Frank Condon

The presence of Miss Dietrich in America seems to be more or less due to certain conclusions formed by studio officials in Hollywood. Looking about them anxiously, the executives apparently decided that there seemed to be in their studio what one might delicately term a dearth of limbs. To be sure, they had fairly presentable limbs already on contract. Nobody has ever been heard finding fault with the underpinning of Clara Bow, Nancy Carroll or Ruth Chatterton, but, nevertheless, the destiny guiders looked yearningly about and sighed.

By mere chance, Josef von Sternberg, the famous director of *The Salvation Hunters,* hied him aboard a steamer and sailed on vacation for Germany, where he kept his

eyes open. He discovered Miss Dietrich, an actress with a modicum of renown, but only a small modicum, and to his delight, which he knew would be his studio's delight, too, she appeared to have exactly the type of limbs that cause pedestrians to stop suddenly on the sidewalk in front of enlarged photographs. So Mr. Von Sternberg forthwith made a movie in Germany with Marlene, which was called *The Blue Angel.* This was the first of the Dietrich experiments, and it was shown in Germany to the plaudits of the multitude. Since then she has appeared in two others, *Morocco* and *Dishonored,* both made in Hollywood, and upon these three reposes her claim to fat stipends and the adulation of young and old.

It is odd to reflect that just a brief while ago, a young German miss was strolling about Germany, probably eating sauerkraut and brocklewurst, and in no time at all her name shrieks at Broadway and other Broadways in signs that must cost plenty of money a kilowatt hour.

Marlene's calm is astonishing, especially when the action is snapping all about her and most women you know would be standing on one foot and shrieking to heaven. There is always present among beholders a feeling that Miss Dietrich may at any moment let go and explode, or burst into flames and burn away the front-row seats before the gratified auditors can get out of the building. So far, this threat has been confined to a promise.

Almost the first happy look Americans had at the new German star—and she wasn't a star then at all—was a bit of a thing the movies call a trailer, by which they mean a forerunner or promise of something to come. This trailer introduced Marlene in a charming, informal costume, the sort of boudoiry thing in which married men think other men's wives would look rather snappy. A brisk comedian led her into her introduction, asking her jolly questions, and almost immediately it was observed that the studio officials needed to worry about limbs no longer. That problem was solved, as everyone could and did see, and the delighted spectators leaned forward and heard Marlene say in a pleasant voice that she could speak English, and when further pressed by the comic fellow as to whether she possessed that nameless quality called It, beheld her gesture lightly and swish the eloquent robe she wore in a way to leave no doubt at all.   *(1931)*

Marlene (here in The Garden of Allah, *1937), as cool as they come—onscreen. At '20s idol John Gilbert's funeral, she wept, wailed and staggered out of the chapel.*

Open Minds
by Ron Cooper

No one who has watched any scene they made during their 18 years as a team could doubt that Laurel and Hardy operated as two minds without a single thought.

Who else but Stan Laurel could saunter up to a soda fountain and innocently ask for "mustachio" ice cream?

Who else but fat, pompous Oliver Hardy could break the icy silence with a lady on a stagecoach by observing, amid blushes and tie-twiddles, "Awful lot of weather we're having . . ."?

English-born Stan Laurel directed and edited many of the team's more than 100 pictures. Oliver Hardy labeled Stan, whom he seldom saw off-screen, the genius of the duo. They won an Oscar in 1932 for The Music Box.

Together, they bounce and blunder off each other to set new standards for mindlessness. Like the time Stan takes Ollie's temperature. Shoving a huge "thermometer" in the (typically) open mouth, Stan pulls it out and shakes it.

Confusion and silence. "Well?" says Ollie. After a long double-take, Stan shrugs and blurts, "Wet and Windy."

"Yoouu IDIOT!" Ollie booms. "That's a barometer!"

In appearance and mannerisms, they were an elegant mismatch. Skinny Stan Laurel, wearing his hair in a vertical shock mop, played the well-meaning dim-wit. Oliver Hardy, rotund, with greasy bangs and a slow-burn stare, affected normality. *(1971)*

On The Road

by Bob Hope

At the Paramount studio I met Billy Selwyn, the assistant producer assigned to the film. He greeted me with, "You're a very lucky fellow. Wait until you hear the number Leo Robin and Ralph Ranger have written for you to sing with Shirley Ross in this picture."

He took me over to the studio music room and played a recording of "Thanks for the Memory" for me. It sounded so beautiful that I asked if I could borrow it to play for my wife at the hotel, where we were staying.

When I played it for her, she listened and said, "I don't think it's so much."

"It's a terrific number," I protested.

"Not to me, it isn't," she said. Dolores is a wonderful

girl; she's both the salt and the pepper of the earth. But she's only human, and being human, she makes human mistakes. When I tell her this she stares at her wedding ring; then looks at me, and I know what she's thinking.

In 1931 I went back into vaudeville once more, dovetailing it with picture-house work. Then, in 1932, I met God's gift to the Crosbys. I first saw Bing near The Friars club on 48th Street, just before I opened at the Capitol. Bing was on the Cremo radio program. Two months later we were both booked into the Capitol with Abe Lyman and his orchestra.

The big electric sign hanging before the Capitol spelled *Bing Crosby and Bob Hope,* just as it's been spelled out many times since on the marquee of the Paramount and other theaters. I was the emcee, and after Bing sang his songs, we had fun clowning. We did our impression of two orchestra leaders meeting in the street. Each of us pulled out a baton and led the other while he talked, as if leading an orchestra. Next, we did our impression of two farmers meeting. One of us asked, "How are things down on the farm?" The other said, "It's pretty cold in the reading room." Then we milked each other's thumbs. Real Noel Coward stuff. It was the beginning of a long, pleasant and profitable association.

In 1939, *The Cat and the Canary,* with Paulette Goddard, was the picture that really broke the ice for me as far as audience acceptance was concerned. Paramount has always been fair to me. As soon as I became a greater draw, they paid me more. All I had to do was ask them for it in a threatening way, and it didn't tire me out to ask.

After *The Cat and the Canary,* I went into the first Road picture, *The Road to Singapore,* with Bing. The Road pictures grew out of a typical Hollywood switch— one of those it-starts-out-to-be-this-then-somebody-gets-a-brighter-idea affairs. Originally there had been a picture called *The Road to Mandalay.* Harlan Thompson was all set to be its producer. Who wrote the original version of *The Road to Mandalay* I don't know, but two Paramount contract writers, Frank Butler and Don Hartman, did a rewrite job on it. They changed it from serious to funny— they had George Burns and Gracie Allen in mind for it—and it was retitled *The Road to Singapore.* Burns and Allen proved unavailable and the next idea was to star Fred MacMurray and Jack Oakie in it. When MacMurray

Non-movie activities occupied much of their time—Bing with his golf tourney, Bob with overseas troop visits.

Bob and Bing **On the Road to Utopia**, *destination obviously not yet reached. Bing won an Oscar, sold over 400 million records before his death on a golf course in 1977.*

and Oakie were lost because of a previous commitment, Bing and I were tapped.

They used the name "Singapore" because Don and Frank didn't think "Mandalay" sounded treacherous enough. As Don put it, "You can take a piece of used chewing gum and flip it at a map, and wherever it sticks you can lay a Road picture, so long as the people who live there are the kind of jokers who cook and eat strangers. If they're nasty and menacing, it'll be a good Road picture. The key to the whole thing is menace offsetting the humor."

There was no thought, however, that that first Road picture would develop into a series. It became a series when a writer named Sy Bartlett came in with a story about two fellows who were trekking through the jungles of Madagascar. The catch was that a movie named *Stanley and Livingston* had just been released and was so similar to Bartlett's that it ruined it. Bartlett's story was a highly dramatic one, but Don Hartman took it, gagged it up and named it *The Road to Zanzibar*.

Most of the Road pictures have the same plot: Crosby chasing Lamour, me chasing Crosby, and the public right behind us—gaining all the time. Dorothy is my nomination for one of the bravest gals in motion pictures. She stands there before the camera and ad-libs with Crosby and me, knowing that the way the script is written she'll come up second or third best in the end. But she fears nothing. She adds to the fun of the goings on by coming on the set with her teeth blacked out, and she should be decorated for patience because, when Bing and I are working out our

lines for the next take, Dottie just stands there and listens. Once in a while she'll say, "How about a line for me?" This usually brings a fast "Quiet, honey. All we want you to do is to look beautiful and twirl your sarong!"

Those routines in which Bing and I rib each other began as a peg upon which both of us could hang our jokes. We started to give each other the needle when we rehearsed our radio shows together. When he called "Clabber" and I called him "Lard Belly" or "Blubber" or "Dad," it drew laughs from the bystanders and the crew. It occurred to us that that kind of ribbing might amuse a wide audience, and we gradually worked our verbal jabs into the show itself.

As an extra refinement upon this technique, we developed a kind of boring-from-within trick, an infiltration-behind-the-lines stunt. Our writers would say to Bing, "When he calls you 'Fatty,' you say to him, 'That's not exactly baby fat you've got there yourself. I happen to know that Sophie Tucker lends you her cast-off girdles.'" Then they'd come to me, tell me what Bing was going to say, and suggest, "Right ahead of his line you say, 'And don't pull that ancient wheeze about Sophie Tucker's girdles. There's no bounce left in the joke or the girdles.'" This piece of skulduggery left Bing standing there with his script in his hand, wondering how he'd been double-crossed.

He got even for that in a scene I did with him in *The Road to Rio*. The scene was a superdramatic one, with me down on my knees clutching at his coat and saying, "Don't leave me! Don't leave me!" When I finished the first take, Bing pulled the Oscar he'd won for *Going My Way* from under his coat and presented it to me. It amused the visitors on the set. I think he'd arranged for an extra large number of them to be there. *(1954)*

Double Dealers
by Milton Krims

As if you didn't already know, there is much talk today of credibility gaps, put-ons and rip-offs. The con game, we are told, is a way of life and respectability, a measure of survival. We hear that morality is a reflexive preoccupation and virtue a subjective exercise. Today's disciplines—especially psychology and sociology—provide computerized conclusions about current social ailments, undoubtedly valuable as statistics. But how much do they really tell us about the individual human being? Even the computer is not equipped to explore every living cell in the immeasurably vast body of society. And even if it could, it does not speak in the simple, nonscientific language of the people.

For successful communication with our times, we turn to the arts . . . the painter, the writer (collectively), the theater, films. The scientist is pragmatic, justifiably concerned with the end result, the revelation that ends, after long and often tedious research, with success or failure. The artist is instinctive, offers the facts of the human situation as he sees them, hoping he will lead his audience through reflection to revelation, never forgetting his first responsibility is to entertain. For without entertainment there is no audience and without audience the artist wastes his endeavor on emptiness.

All of which is intended as preface to discussion of a film titled *The Sting*. It's about a "big con," meaning a swindle involving sizable money, success depending on imagination, ingenuity, courage and expert psychological manipulation to lead the "mark" (victim) to the "sting" (taking his money). It is from first to last a total "put-on," contriving people into places and postures with the felicitous ease of a "Mission Impossible" charade . . . except that it has good reason for being and most of the time makes good sense. And much suspense. It is a kind of filmic reflection that leads to post-film revelation . . . if one is of a mind to update its well-hidden admonitions and precautions.

A big con is a meticulously planned extravaganza as carefully staged as any top theatrical production. To begin, the mark must be studied for his weaknesses. Doyle Lonnegan, rich and powerful racketeer, ruthless disciplinarian, congenitally suspicious, has a weakness for poker and is a notoriously bad loser . . . which is why he is a compulsive cheater, as adept as any grifter at dealing from the bottom of the deck. This indicates the wire game as most likely to succeed. Success depends on convincing

him that his newfound friends have a way of delaying race results to bookie joints, thus giving him a sure-thing bet on a completed race before the bookie even knows the race has started. This, in turn, necessitates setting up a "store," a replica of a well-established, efficiently functioning and flashy bookmaker's room crowded with prosperous people making, winning and losing large bets. All this takes money. And they're all quite short at this moment. But love will find a way.

It is a delightful irony that the mark himself pays for the setup. How is for you to see; enough to say cheater Lonnegan is outcheated by cheater Gondorff with money picked from Lonnegan's own pocket, thus creating complications about the payoff, which brings Hooker into the situation with an offer to double-cross his partner Gondorff because he wants the joint for his own. And he knows just how to do it. (See wire game, above.) Lonnegan nibbles . . . and the game begins.

Paul Newman and Robert Redford are wonderfully convincing (and droll) as two practitioners of the gentle art of separating a sucker from his money, playing the game with purposeful charm, insouciant good humor and persuasive flimflammery. That they are unmitigated, conscienceless scoundrels enjoying every ploy of the big con is of secondary consideration; after all, their intent is commendable and there is no harm in cheating a cheater, especially when the cheater is Robert Shaw, who stalks through the deception with exquisite nastiness. I realize this is not a recommended moral attitude. However, in today's world, I am often led to wonder what is.

The screenplay by David S. Ward is sharply definitive, colorfully dialogued and tightly structured. I found the very last "put-on" disappointing, feeling reality would have given substantive irony to the story. Since it's a surprise, I won't discuss it any further. George Roy Hill's direction is precisely lighthearted, keeping pace and people in quick tempo and avoiding the cuteness that so often betrays the validity of the play within the play.

We are told that in recent years "the big con has become less a criminal activity and more the domain of politics and big business." Perhaps *The Sting* should be seen as a historical document reflecting a past that reveals much of the present.   *(1974)*

The four bluest eyes in Hollywood and two of the town's box-office heaviest-weights. Between them, they have five Best Actor nominations, no Oscars.

Our Grace
by Pete Martin

Five years before, when I'd interviewed Grace Kelly in California, she had been completely poised, in control of herself and of our interview. She had worn graciousness and charm like a gown she had put on and forgotten about. Nevertheless a certain inner reserve showed in her eyes when I asked her questions she thought too personal.

To be truthful about it, I'm not adept at asking some kinds of questions—such as, "What do you do about your love life?" Notwithstanding my earlier interview, I had braced myself to ask her a few like that. When I did, her reaction was like nothing I had ever experienced before. She looked at me, smiled and said absolutely nothing. I wouldn't have been startled if she'd changed the subject or had said, "I'd rather not answer that," or, "I am sorry, I'm afraid that's my own affair." But she had done none of those things. She had just given me that long, level look and that silent smile. I felt boorish and crude and I had hurried to erase that silent smile from her face and to find a subject about which she would talk.

Now that I was sitting with her in her burnt-sienna-and-cream-colored palace in Monaco—the palace is definitely not pink, although some reporters, bemused by the alliteration of the words "pink" and "palace," have described it that way—and talking to her once more, I decided that she had changed not an iota since I had talked to her last, in 1954. I had thought then that her bearing was regal, her manner that of a princess. Her poise and the fact that she was unmistakably and unshakably a lady had caused one Hollywood reporter to label her "the girl with the chilled-steel insides." I hadn't found her that way. To me she had been simply a remarkably beautiful young woman who happened to be dedicated to the job of acting.

I found that her manner and her bearing were still poised. She was still gracious. She still wore her charm like a silken gown. But on second thought I decided that perhaps there was an iota of difference. She seemed less tired, less strained than she had been in 1954, when she was about to set out for the Riviera to make *To Catch a Thief* with Cary Grant. Perhaps there was another difference too—if anything, she was even more beautiful than she was in her Hollywood days.

"What about the crowds of admirers when you and your husband travel?" I asked Princess Grace. "Don't they get a little burdensome on occasion? Do they push and shove you and your family?"

"Often," she said. "But it's not as bad now as it was

during the first year or two after our marriage, although even then the people were very kind to us—at least they threw kisses instead of tomatoes. However, there was one terrible time in the rain in Genoa when the pressure of the crowd was so great the side of our car was pushed in. It was frightening."

"You mean you could actually see it being pushed out of shape?" I asked her.

"There was a crushing sound," she said. "I could hear it. But the most frightening thing about it was that when a car is pushed in upon itself in that way, the people pinned against it are helpless. They can be squashed too."

Among my own friends who had stopped off in Monte Carlo was Bob Hope. I had asked him if he'd seen the prince and princess. "They asked me over to the palace at seven o'clock," he'd said. "They came down from their place in the country to be there. You know, this guy has a great sense of humor. I was impressed with the prince. He's a regular, down-to-earth sort. One thing that tickled me was all those little cards he had placed over the bar in the palace. One of them said, DON'T PUT OFF UNTIL TO-MORROW WHAT YOU CAN DO THE DAY AFTER TOMORROW. We just sat around and told jokes and helped the princess make the drinks. I said to her, 'Everybody wanted to know what I was going to call you, and I told them I was going to call you our Grace.'

"There were no flunkies at our elbows," Hope went on. "We went behind the bar and did it ourselves. I was really impressed when the princess said to me, 'You know who I was thinking about the other day? Barney Dean.' Barney was my friend and Bing's friend. He came on the *Road to Singapore* set one day selling Christmas cards, and Bing and I got him a job writing gags because he had such a wonderful sense of humor, and he was such a lovable little guy with a great personality. The fact that Grace remembered Barney knocked me out, because while he was a little fellow we all loved, I didn't think she'd give him a thought in her new life. But she hasn't changed. She's just as much fun as she used to be at Paramount and she is so thoughtful and considerate of the prince. She made sure he understood the background of everything we were talking about. If you ask me, those two have a very warm relationship."   *(1960)*

If serene Grace Kelly were not the daughter of a million-aire, her marriage to Monaco-esque Prince Rainier would be the perfect Cinderella story.

Dimpled Diplomat

by Barbara Kevles

We have been talking so long that we are the only customers left; so, after leaving a gargantuan tip, Shirley leads me to a place I never knew existed—the Junior League Lounge in the Waldorf-Astoria, replete with marble fireplace, terrace and antiques. Almost at once, Shirley receives a call from the White House, which she takes right there so I can't help overhearing her concluding line, "If Henry will do it, tell him I'll change my lifestyle."

Sensing my wide-eyed curiosity about this last remark, she launches into an anecdote, prefacing it with, "Well, Henry tells this story . . ." recounting how at a White House dinner commemorating the U.N.'s 25th Anniversary, Henry Kissinger requested she be seated next to him and how she tried to persuade him to bring the Vietnam War before the Security Council by having him read the worn miniature U.N. Charter she had in her evening purse (which "I carry every place I go") and how he had to stop eating to look over the marked pages. "If we paid attention to these articles we could avoid wars," and she smiles, "or get out of those we were in." How Kissinger obliged, jesting. "I wanted to sit next to the youngest woman invited and what does she have me do, read a *book*!"   *(1972)*

Shirley and Bill "Bojangles" Robinson made six movies together; Bill taught her to dance in the memorable staircase sequence from The Little Colonel. *Onscreen since 1932 (at age five), Shirley made her last movie in 1949.*

Smile, You're On...

(Left) The reining princess of the cinema takes a royal ride. Lately, however, the dimpled darling has traded ponies for protocol.

(Left) A bespectacled Archibald Leach with woman friend. Could she possibly be the legendary "Judy, Judy, Judy"? (Above) Liz, here on location, fields questions from the press, responding with a puzzled, "Richard who?"

(Right) The two finalists in the Gorgeous Gams contest held at the Hollywood Canteen compare equipment. (Below) Between movie roles, Bette sometimes moonlighted as a department-store mannequin.

(Above) A young Kate Hepburn, with friend, dispels the rumors that she is hard to get along with. (Right) America's number-one pinup girl dances with America's favorite movie gangster.

Last Time Around

by Theodore Taylor and James Atwater

For over 30 years Paul Mantz had been a daredevil stunt pilot who had been unable to turn down the tough assignments. He had flown under bridges, smashed his airplane head-on into another, clipped off wings by flying between two trees. He was the man who had crash-landed a B-17 in *Twelve o'Clock High*, and he was the man who had skimmed a Stearman through a hangar in *It's a Mad, Mad, Mad, Mad World*. So when producer-director Robert Aldrich approached him earlier this year, Mantz decided to postpone his retirement for one more stunt.

Aldrich needed Mantz for a tricky bit of flying that was absolutely necessary to make the audiences believe a most unbelievable movie he was making for 20th Century-Fox

Movie stunt men are a special breed. They live dangerously, and some die young, on the job, before cameras that record an image of real death in glorious Technicolor. Paul Mantz was not young. He was 61 and planning to retire when the bosses asked him to fly by just once more. To the surprise of no one who knew him, he did not refuse.

called *Flight of the Phoenix*. In one wild, climactic scene, with some men strapped to the wings, the *Phoenix* struggles into the air and manages to fly to civilization.

It was the kind of scene that would have to be done live. Mantz would have the job, essentially, of taking an aircraft purposely designed to look as though it would not fly at all and making it fly—barely.

On the morning of July 6 Mantz finally took off to try the stunt, but had to turn back when his engine overheated. The next day Mantz coaxed the *Phoenix* into the air again, and several times dipped into Buttercup Valley, touched his wheels down, and made it out. But when Mantz landed, he discovered that he had been too close to the camera. They wanted another try.

At 6:10 on the morning of July 7, Mantz strapped on his cloth helmet and said, "Well, here we go again." He sounded weary. In the rear cockpit was another old man, Buddy Rose, 64, who used to walk wings in flying circuses.

Mantz made one pass. It was good. On his second pass, Mantz touched down the *Phoenix* twice and barely cleared the western dunes. It was excellent. He circled while the directors of the scene radioed him their congratulations. Then they asked him to do it one last time. They wanted what the trade calls a "protection" shot, in case something happened to the first. For three decades directors had been congratulating Mantz, then asking for one more.

Now, anxious to get the whole thing over, he agreed. His voice came booming over the radio: "I'll give them a good one. That will be the last one."

They put out a white flag to guide him in. For a moment he was out of sight as he circled around the dunes, and then he was coming again. "I think I see it," he radioed, and you could almost see him leaning forward slightly and squinting through his glasses. Then he was over the dunes and down into the valley and saying triumphantly, "I see it—I see it," and touching down. He hit once and rose into the air for 100 feet. Then he bounced, heavily. His wheels broke through the crust of sand, but he wobbled back into the air. He gunned his Pratt & Whitney engine with a great roar to get the nose up and the tail down.

It was the right thing to do, of course, but it was no use. The absurdly long fuselage was beginning to break in two. Seconds later, the prop dug into the sand, and the pieces began to somersault along the floor of the valley. Buddy Rose lived through it. Paul Mantz died in the sand. *(1965)*

Farewell, Great Lover

by Beverly Smith, Jr.

The mania began with the first showing of a silent film called *The Sheik* in 1921. Valentino played the lead: a romantic Arab chieftain, passionate, masterful, irresistible. He snatched Agnes Ayres from her steed. "Stop struggling, you little fool," flashed the subtitle. Hot stuff. Overnight he became a star.

A press agent high on Greek mythology had Valentino present a golden apple to the more beautiful of his two co-stars in Cobra, *Nita Naldi and Gertrude Olmsted.*

The adoration increased with each succeeding film of the great lover. With the appearance of *The Son of the Sheik* in 1926, the Valentino worship became feverish.

On the morning of August sixteenth came the shocking news, on the front page of even the staid *New York Times*, that the handsome thirty-one-year-old star had been rushed to a hospital in New York for critical surgery—appendix and ulcers. In the next few days the bulletins were reassuring. Then, front page again: *PERITONITIS FEARED,*

CONDITION ALARMING. On Monday, August twenty-third, huge headlines: *VALENTINO DEAD! THOU-SANDS OUTSIDE HOSPITAL WEEP AND PRAY*. The stories from Hollywood said that Pola Negri, who recently had announced her engagement to Valentino, was pros-trated by grief, with two physicians trying to control her hysteria.

On that Tuesday evening Grace and I met for dinner in a small Italian restaurant in Greenwich Village. We had *scaloppine*, washed down with what was called "red ink." This was supposed to be a wine of the Chianti family, but the kinship was not close.

Cheered by the wine, I looked forward to an entertain-ing and instructive evening. "Well, Grace," I said, "what's the journalism lesson for tonight?"

"I'm afraid it's pretty gruesome," she said. "They've got poor Valentino laid out for public view in the Gold Room at Campbell's Funeral Church—Broadway and 66th. They've rigged him up in full evening dress in a fancy silver casket. My city editor says the fans are putting on a regular mob scene outside, scuffling to get in. The pressure of the crowd pushed in one of Campbell's big plate-glass windows. Three cops, a photographer and some of the women were cut so badly by the glass that they had to be taken to the hospital. It sounds kind of ghastly—I don't want to drag you into this."

It also sounded kind of dangerous, I said. A girl could get hurt in a mob like that. This was the very time she needed a man's strength and judgment. "I will protect you," I said.

As we came up from the subway, we saw a dense column of people, mostly women, shuffling southward along the east side of Broadway toward the funeral parlor

Mustachioed and unknown, young Valentino poses for a picture prior to leaving his native Italy.

six blocks away. Police kept them in line. From the other side of the street an even larger crowd, straining against the police lines, was struggling to dash across and break into the column which was approaching the Mecca of mourn-ing. Every now and then a group of frantic women would elude the foot patrolmen and make a wild rush, only to be turned back by mounted police.

Now a veteran sergeant of foot police intercepted us. "Where you think you're going?" he demanded. Grace showed him her reporter's card. He softened. "The Brook-lyn *Eagle*, huh? I was born and raised in Flatbush. Whole family used to read the *Eagle*. What can I do for you?"

"The editors want me to go into the Gold Room where the casket is," Grace said apologetically. "You know—get the atmosphere."

"It's awful in there, miss," said the sergeant gloomily. "Women screeching and fainting. No place for a nice young lady like you. But—well, seeing you're from the *Eagle*, I guess I can slip you in. How about this guy—er—this gent'man with you. He a reporter?"

"Not yet," Grace said. "He's my husband."

"Then he can't go in—sorry—not unless he goes back about ten blocks and stands in line three or four hours. Then you might not find him again all night, not in this mob. Tell you what, mister," he said, turning to me. "You stand on the northeast corner over there, in that space we've cleared by the lamppost. You got my permission. Stay right there until your wife gets back."

For ten minutes or so I stood on my corner, leaning on my umbrella and trying to look inconspicuous. Then the mounted patrolman guarding my sector, cantering back after helping repel another feminine charge a half block to the south, spotted me. He reined in his horse and glared. "Hey, you!" he shouted. "How'd you sneak over there? Get back across the street."

"I'm waiting here for my wife," I yelled back, standing firm.

The ridiculous excuse seemed to exasperate him. He touched the flank of his horse and rode straight at me. I dodged instinctively and dashed out into the street.

The cop rode at me again. "I got permission to stand here!" I yelled. "From the sergeant." I'm not sure he heard me above the tumult. If he did, he paid no heed. Again I dodged, ran, feinted, ducked.

As I once more sprinted safely back to my post, I heard a louder roar from the crowd. They were cheering me.

There is something stimulating in the cheers of the multitude, however irrational. I caught my second wind and went on with the game. My triumph did not last long. As I dodged and weaved, I heard the ominous clop-clop of hoofs converging from north and south—reinforcements coming up.

My original pursuer vaulted down from his saddle. He seized my arm. "You're under arrest," he growled. As he led me away, the crowd booed.   *(1962)*

Rodolfo Alfonzo Raffaelo Pierre Filibert Guglielmi Di Valentina D'Antonguolla was a landscape gardener and dishwasher before his transformation into The Sheik.

It's Academic, Uncle Oscar

If you want to be taken seriously, give yourself an award—or arrange to have someone else, under your subtle guidance, make the presentation. In May, 1927, pursuing such logic, 36 leaders of the burgeoning film industry convened in Los Angeles to organize the Academy of Motion Picture Arts and Sciences, and a short time later held a banquet at which Louis B. Mayer suggested that they focus attention on cinematic achievements by presenting awards of merit.

One of the first to agree with Mayer was actor Conrad Nagel: "Whatever we give, it should be a symbol of continuing progress—militant, dynamic." Art director Cedric Gibbons, wasting no time in furthering Nagel's ideas,

sketched on a tablecloth the figure of a stalwart man, standing on a reel of film and holding a crusader's sword. Thus, Oscar came to be, although he didn't get his name until four years later when Margaret Herrick, retired executive director of the Academy, saw the statuette and noted, "Why, he looks like my Uncle Oscar." In the next room a big-eared reporter overheard the remark and later wrote: "Academy employees have affectionately dubbed their famous gold statuette 'Oscar.' " Imagine the situation had Margaret Herrick's uncle been named Absolom. Or Bucky.

In that first year, it was January, 1929, before ballots were cast for film performances during the year ending July 31, 1928. The results were published in February, and the first presentations made at the Hollywood Roosevelt Hotel, on May 16, when 15 golden statuettes were presented by Academy President Douglas Fairbanks and Vice-President William C. De Mille, chairman of the program. All of the winners were men except a young actress named Janet Gaynor, who was honored for her work in three pictures: *Sunrise, Seventh Heaven* and *Street Angel*.

During this first year, the Academy recognized the need for special Honorary Awards, two of which were given—to Warner Brothers for the pioneer talking picture *The Jazz Singer*; and to Charles Chaplin for his four-star accomplishment in producing, directing, writing and starring in *The Circus*. The list of achievements honored was reduced to seven—two for acting and one each for Best Picture, Directing, Writing, Cinematography and Art Direction.

In 1932, Short Subject Awards were introduced, with Walt Disney making the first of many trips to the podium to receive an Oscar for the year's Best Cartoon—and an honorary statuette for creating Mickey Mouse. Before his death in 1966, Disney won an Irving Thalberg Award, three more Honorary Awards and 24 more Oscars, for a grand total of 30—considerably more than any other individual in Academy history. At the 1939 presentations he received an Honorary Oscar for Snow White and seven little ones for the dwarfs.

Self-confidence is surely one of the prerequisites for Hollywood success, but in 1934 it was precisely that attribute that resulted in Frank Capra's near-terminal embarrassment. He had received his first Best Director nomi-

The Academy has yet to present Bob with an award for a film appearance. "Well, maybe next year," Bob hopes.

"For his contribution to the laughter of the world. . ." Bob Hope received a lifetime membership from the Academy in 1944.

Gish began with Griffith, still works in movies, won special Oscar for special contributions.

nation (later he would win three times) that year, and at the award presentations when master of ceremonies Will Rogers said "Come and get it, Frank," Capra got up and started for the rostrum. He had gone about 40 feet when he realized that Rogers was motioning to Frank Lloyd, who won for his work in *Cavalcade*. Capra later described his return to his seat as "the longest crawl in history."

In 1935, Columbia's *It Happened One Night* won across the board, with awards going to Capra, Claudette Colbert and Clark Gable. Not expecting to win, Miss Colbert was boarding a train for New York at the moment she was announced as a winner of the Best Actress Award. At the last minute, she was taken from the train and hurried by taxi to the Biltmore Hotel where the show was in progress. Irvin S. Cobb interrupted a presentation to Shirley Temple to give Miss Colbert her Oscar (Shirley Temple's Oscar was the first Honorary Award for Juveniles).

Two years later, at the 1937 show, Oscars were given

Oscar night means stargazing in more than 24,000,000 homes in America. Millions more around the world hear, "And the winner is" via a corps of 500 journalists.

Ol' Blue Eyes and Uncle Oscar got together as result of Frank's supporting role in **From Here to Eternity***: compensation for not rolling in the surf with Deborah Kerr.*

for the first time in recognition of the Best Supporting Actor and Supporting Actress. The next year, Luise Rainer was voted Best Actress for *The Great Ziegfeld*, being the first player to win an Oscar two years in a row.

The first Irving G. Thalberg Memorial Award, presented in 1938 for consistently high quality of production, went to Darryl F. Zanuck. The next year, Special Effects Awards were introduced and Twentieth Century-Fox took the honors with *The Rains Came*.

During the war, the Oscar statuettes were made of plaster, since metal was an essential war material. The plaster Oscars given during the four war years were exchanged for metal ones after the war. Winners of these first plaster Oscars given in 1943 included Jimmy Cagney for *Yankee Doodle Dandy*, Greer Garson for *Mrs. Miniver* and supporting actress Teresa Wright for *Mrs. Miniver*. Miss Wright was also nominated that year in the Best Actress Category for her work in *Pride of the Yankees*. Director William Wyler's wife accepted his award for *Mrs. Miniver*, since Major Wyler was leading a bombing raid on Germany that night.

The 1943 ceremony was the last to be staged at a banquet. Hollywood considered it ridiculous to dine on chicken under glass when food was being rationed elsewhere. The 1944 program was held at Grauman's Chinese Theater and Oscars were given to *Casablanca*, Paul Lukas for *Watch on the Rhine*, Jennifer Jones for *The Song of Bernadette* and Charles Coburn for *The More the Merrier*.

The entire program went on network radio for the first time the following year. *Going My Way* was voted the Best Picture, and won acting awards for Bing Crosby and Barry Fitzgerald (supporting actor) and the directing award for Leo McCarey. Fitzgerald was up for both Best Actor and Best Supporting Actor awards for the same role. Rules were then adopted to prevent this from happening again.

Ingrid Bergman was voted Best Actress for *Gaslight* and Ethel Barrymore Best Supporting Actress for *None but the Lonely Heart*. This made Lionel and Ethel Barrymore the only brother and sister to win Oscars.

In 1946 the big winner was *The Lost Weekend*, which also brought Oscars to its star, Ray Milland, and its director, Billy Wilder. James Dunn won a supporting award for *A Tree Grows in Brooklyn*; Anne Revere, for *National Velvet*.

Joan Crawford missed the suspense of the actual ceremonies that year because she was sick in bed when her name was announced as Best Actress for *Mildred Pierce*.

It's unlikely that any Academy Awards presentation will provide a moment to match the poignancy of the 1947 Ceremonies, when Harold Russell won two Awards for his role in *The Best Years of Our Lives*.

He held them proudly aloft in his two artificial hands when he stepped from the podium after being honored as Best Supporting Actor and receiving a special Honorary

Oscar for bringing hope and courage to his fellow veterans.

In Academy records, the year 1960 is remembered for *Ben Hur*, the film that set an all-time record for Awards—a total of 11—which included Best Picture, Art Directing, Cinematography, Costume Design, Film Editing, Directing (William Wyler), Music Score and Sound. Charlton Heston was named Best Actor.

The Awards Program was presented in a new theater in 1969, the Dorothy Chandler Pavilion of the Los Angeles Music Center, where Katharine Hepburn won her third Oscar for *The Lion in Winter*—a record for an actress in a leading role.

The years that followed were marked by a number of Award firsts, among them the first program telecast in color (1966), the first Academy Gold Medal going to master of ceremonies Bob Hope (1966), and the first telecast live, worldwide, by communications satellite (1969).

Then in April, 1972, arrived perhaps the most memorable scene in the history of the Awards—the presentation of an Honorary Award to Charles Chaplin "for the incalculable effect he has had in making motion pictures the art form of this century." Chaplin, who at 83 had returned to Hollywood after a 20-year absence, was given an unprecedented standing ovation.

Those who were watching and somehow survived dry-eyed through the clips from Chaplin's films had to break down when the small, white-haired man in the center of the stage himself began to cry. Everyone, including all of those gathered with him on the stage, joined in singing "Smile," a song he had composed. The 50th birthday of Oscar was still five years in the future, but it would be hard to imagine a more fitting celebration.

Acknowledgments

Text

All selections in this book first appeared in *The Saturday Evening Post*. Copyright © 1902, 1909, 1922, 1926, 1928, 1930, 1931, 1932, 1933, 1936, 1937, 1938, 1939, 1941, 1942, 1943, 1945, 1947, 1948, 1949, 1950, 1951, 1952, 1953, 1954, 1955, 1956, 1957, 1960, 1961, 1963, 1964, 1965, 1966, 1968, 1971, 1974 The Curtis Publishing Company.

The editors wish to thank the authors and their heirs and agents who have graciously cooperated with us in the republication of this material. Our special thanks to Pete Martin for permission to reprint portions of his interviews with Ingrid Bergman, Gary Cooper, Clark Gable, Cary Grant, Alfred Hitchcock, Grace Kelly, Marilyn Monroe, Jimmy Stewart and John Wayne.

"Babylon Revisited" by F. Scott Fitzgerald is reprinted from TAPS AT REVEILLE with the permission of Charles Scribner's Sons. Copyright 1931 The Curtis Publishing Company.

Excerpts from MURDER IN THE CALAIS COACH by Agatha Christie reprinted by permission of Harold Ober Associates, Inc. Copyright 1933 by Agatha Christie. Renewed.

Excerpt from TRUE GRIT by Charles Portis reprinted by permission of Simon & Schuster, a Division of Gulf & Western Corporation. Copyright © 1968 by Charles Portis.

Excerpt from COMMODORE HORNBLOWER by C. S. Forester reprinted by permission of Harold Matson Company, Inc. Copyright 1945 The Curtis Publishing Company. Copyright renewed © 1972 by Dorothy E. Forester.

Excerpt from THE SEA OF GRASS by Conrad Richter reprinted by permission of Alfred A. Knopf, Inc. Copyright 1937 The Curtis Publishing Company, and renewed © 1965 by Conrad Richter.

Excerpt from "The Devil and Daniel Webster" reprinted from THE SELECTED WORKS OF STEPHEN VINCENT BENÉT with the permission of Brandt & Brandt. Copyright 1936 The Curtis Publishing Company. Copyright renewed 1964 by Thomas C. Benét, Stephanie B. Mahin and Rachel B. Lewis.

Excerpt from TUGBOAT ANNIE by Norman Reilly Raine reprinted by permission of Elizabeth Raine. Copyright 1931 The Curtis Publishing Company. Copyright renewed 1959 by Elizabeth Raine.

Illustrations

The illustrations on the cover and on pages iii, 5, 15, 33, 67, 75, 87, 91, 93, 95, 98-99, 103, 115 and 141 are reproduced from the pages of *The Saturday Evening Post*. Copyright © 1922, 1928, 1930, 1931, 1932, 1934, 1935, 1936, 1938, 1939, 1952, 1957, 1968, 1977 The Curtis Publishing Company.

Photographs

The Bettmann Archive, Inc. vii, viii, 2, 11, 12, 16, 17, 27, 29, 37, 38 (top), 40, 41, 44, 57, 89, 104, 105, 106, 116, 122, 125, 143 (top right), 145, 146—Black Star 24 (Sipa Press), 42 (John Launois), 120 (Robert Cohen), 132 (Gene Daniels)—Peter C. Borsari 119, 147—Brown Brothers 3, 4, 8, 9, 13, 18, 50, 51, 52, 53, 92, 97, 126, 129, 133, 142 (top left)—Camera 5 45 (Richard Howard)—Culver Pictures, Inc. viii (top), 12, 19, 20, 23, 25, 34, 35, 38 (bottom), 58, 69, 71, 73, 77, 81, 83, 111, 113, 114, 118, 122, 128, 134, 140, 142 (bottom left and bottom right), 143 (top left, bottom left, bottom right)—Harshe, Rotman, & Drucke 148, 150, 151—Magnum 108 (Henri Cartier-Bresson), 139 (Eve Arnold)—Collection of Pete Martin 8—Metropolitan Museum of Art/Film Stills Archive i, 1, 27, 48, 49—NBC-TV 79—National Cowboy Hall of Fame 21—Paramount iv—Springer/Bettmann Film Archive 30, 39, 102, 107, 116, 120—Twentieth Century-Fox 84, 85, 144—Universal Studios 137—Walt Disney Productions 53—Wide World Photos 26, 28, 101, 109.